Praise for *MWF Seeking BFF* by Rachel Bertsche

"Friendship is one of the most important elements of a happy life—but it can be tough to make new friends. In *MWF Seeking BFF,* Rachel Bertsche weaves together engaging and often hilarious adventures in search of a new best friend with the latest research about the science of friendship. I couldn't put it down."
—GRETCHEN RUBIN, author of *The Happiness Project*

"Funny, forthright, and honest as a midnight phone call, Bertsche's zesty hosanna to female bonding defines what it is to be a double-X Millennial." —SHEILA WELLER, author of *Girls Like Us*

"Reading about Rachel Bertsche's search for that special someone, you'll find yourself thinking about all the friends you've ever had—and the ones you hope are right around the corner. Bertsche writes with engaging humor and a measure of poignancy, too. You'll enjoy joining her on the journey."
—JEFFREY ZASLOW, author of *The Girls from Ames*

"Genuine, funny and thoroughly inspiring, *MWF Seeking BFF* is a tribute to female friendships and a must-read for anyone who has ever found herself sunk into her couch and scrolling through the phone list feeling like there's no one to call for a last-minute drink or Sunday brunch."
—RACHEL MACHACEK, author of *The Science of Single*

"*MWF Seeking BFF* is funny, charming, and so relatable. Throughout Rachel [Bertsche]'s journey to develop more meaningful, enduring relationships with other women, I found myself wishing she had my number." —ROBYN OKRANT, author of *Living Oprah*

"I guess you could say Rachel [Bertsche] had me at 'Hello'—I found myself totally invested in her honest, earnest, oftentimes hilarious quest for meaningful female friendship. Whether you're actively seeking a 'BFF' yourself or simply recognize the value in making quality connections with other women, *MWF Seeking BFF* underscores the profound rewards we women stand to reap when we simply open up, reach out to one another, and go for it. A smart, fun, and inspiring page-turner that will surely resonate."
—KELLY VALEN, author of *The Twisted Sisterhood*

By Rachel Bertsche

MWF Seeking BFF:
My Yearlong Search for a New Best Friend

Jennifer, Gwyneth & Me:
The Pursuit of Happiness, One Celebrity at a Time

Jennifer, Gwyneth & Me

Jennifer, Gwyneth & Me

The Pursuit of Happiness, One Celebrity at a Time

Rachel Bertsche

Ballantine Books Trade Paperbacks
New York

FOR MATT AND MAGGIE

CONTENTS

INTRODUCTION

I'll always remember the episode of *Friends* when Jennifer Aniston went from cute-enough girl next door to oh-my-God-I-want-her-body hot. The very scene, in fact.

I barely remember my first kiss. I have no memory of receiving my first paycheck. But Jennifer Aniston's sculpted arms? They seared themselves into my brain.

It was the season after the London wedding that wasn't, when Rachel realized she still loved Ross. During the episode in question ("The One with All the Kissing"), Rachel put Monica in charge of all her decisions. In this particular scene, the friends were in the hallway, fighting over whether Rachel should admit her feelings to Ross. She was wearing a strapless, pale yellow dress with embroidered flowers. It wrapped around her like a sausage casing, barely leaving room to breathe. Jennifer's was a body that the treadmill and Zone Diet built. It said: "I've overhauled my body and I look damn good. I worked for these toned arms, this ripped back, these hot legs, and I'm going to flaunt them."

Every time I see that scene (fairly often, thanks to constant reruns) my gaze shifts to my own arms. *Why can't you be more like hers?*

Yes, I speak to my biceps.

Perhaps I sound more like the men who worship at the Aniston altar, the ones who voted her "Sexiest Woman of All Time" in *Men's Health* and named her *GQ*'s inaugural Woman of the Year, than a straight female who considers Taylor Kitsch circa *Friday Night Lights* the pinnacle of sexy. But as women, we seem to check out our own kind more than men do. We're constantly, and certainly to our detriment, comparing ourselves to the bodies in magazines or on TV, at the gym, even in the office.

And if there's anyone we compare ourselves to most, it's Ms. Aniston. According to the 2012 Hollywood's Hottest Looks survey, an annual poll conducted by two L.A. plastic surgeons, Jennifer's body is America's most coveted. A 2011 *Fitness* magazine poll found the same thing—34 percent of respondents said Jen's was the body they most wanted for themselves. In her twenty years in the spotlight, Jennifer has gone from 25-year-old cute and lovable Friend to 45-year-old sex symbol. She was a bit rounder when she first appeared on-screen, her hair slightly less shiny; but over the next decade, she went from TV newbie to capital S mega-Star—the namesake of a haircut (sure, it was named for her character, but those layers framed Jennifer's face), the wife of Brad Pitt (and then, of course, not anymore), and the magazine cover girl guaranteed to fly off the shelves.

This before-our-very-eyes evolution made Jennifer the pinnacle of Everywoman's affections. Her glow, that aura of The Life, feels—almost—for just a split second, attainable. Because we know she was once a tad more regular, and she feels like an old friend, and we watched her become who she is today. In that one yellow-embroidered-dress moment, she went from regular to luminary, and America's obsession kicked in.

If she could do it, maybe we could, too.

I saw Jen once. It was 2006, and she was arriving for an appearance on *The Late Show.* I worked in New York City at the time, across the street from David Letterman's studio. My coworkers used to run downstairs to stand on 53rd Street and watch celebrities arrive. We wouldn't go for just anyone, of course. We were New Yorkers, thankyouverymuch, not *tourists*—too good, we thought, to stand outside for a mere Kirsten Dunst or Toby

Maguire. My friend once stayed late to see Tom Cruise pull up. Not me. I waited along the security gate for one person and one person only. Jennifer. She wore a black button-down shirt and black mini-shorts and heels. She had some serious legs, a fact that didn't go unnoticed by me or by Dave. Before he even said hello on that night's episode, he told her: "You have tremendous legs. Fantastic legs."

In the decade since *Friends* went off the air, Jennifer's status has only gotten greater. "When Aniston transitioned to Movie Star, those TV eyeballs came with her," writes journalist Mickey Rapkin in a 2011 *Elle* profile. "Her body, a potent advertisement for the dual cocktail of Pilates and hard-earned confidence, quickly became the ideal for American women everywhere."

And if she isn't your ideal, some other celebrity probably is. Last week I heard a woman tell a friend that she fired her trainer because he was making her lift too many weights. "I said I wanted to be Eva Longoria," she said. "Does Eva Longoria have bulky arms?"

We want Eva's arms. Jennifer's legs. The Affleck-Garner marriage. Sarah Jessica's style. And it'd be great if we could cook and master cleanse like Gwyneth, herd our six (six!) kids through the airport like Angelina, and keep a stellar career afloat like, well, all of them.

Celebrity culture has become an ever-present beast over the past two decades—a twenty-four-hour stalk-fest that enables me to click through an eighteen-photo slideshow of Reese Witherspoon's body evolution, complete with a "Zoom In" feature—so it's hard not to be consumed with achieving celeb levels of perfection. Or supposed perfection.

Here's the reality: My life, while far from perfect, is good. Great, even. I'm healthy. I have a husband I love dearly who loves me back. Wonderful friends. A supportive family who, aside from the occasional nagging phone call, doesn't drive me too crazy. I've got a steady career that allows me to be my own boss and work from a coffee shop around the corner.

And yet, when I spot a picture of Heidi Klum walking down the street with daughter in one hand, Marc Jacobs bag in the other, and summer scarf tied in that effortlessly cool *what-this-old-thing?* manner, my first thought is this: "Rachel, get your act together."

I've gained seventeen pounds since I got married three years ago. My house is constantly a mess and no matter how many times I clean my room and say "this time for good!" it's messy within hours. I haven't woken up with my alarm in approximately nine months and I think I might actually have a disabling television addiction. I spend the majority of my days dressed in some combination of pajamas and exercise clothes, which are more often than not interchangeable.

I'm not exactly the picture of perfection.

Wait, what's that? Nobody's perfect, you say?

But what about Jennifer?

I kid, I kid. Sort of. I understand that even the Goddess Aniston doesn't exactly have it made. There was the whole Brad-and-Angelina thing, after all. And Heidi Klum nursed a pretty public divorce under that winning smile and effortlessly cool scarf. They've certainly had hard times. And yet these A-listers seem to have that "strength in adversity" image down cold. It's as if that $265 Crème de la Mer face cream actually equips them to weather a storm more resolutely than the rest of us. When I have a truly bad day, I cry in public, often to the awkward discomfort of the Chicago El passengers around me. When Heidi Klum has a rough month, when her iron-clad marriage falls apart for the world to see, she simply muses to the media, "Sometimes I think a curve-ball just comes at you. . . . With my life, my family, my business— I want to go forward."

Perhaps there is actual wisdom infused in those jars of moisturizer.

Here's the thing about celebrities: It doesn't matter to us if their personal lives are perfect or not. No one actually expects to go through life without a couple of bumps and bruises. But aside from the Lindsay Lohans of the world, who seem to ping-pong between rehab and jail, our A-listers hide their troubles so well. They might lose a loved one, or a job, and you'll see those trials in the headlines, but never on their faces. No matter what's going on behind the scenes (and how are we Average Janes to know what happens behind closed doors?) they still embody that image of perfection.

And we still want to be just like them.

Because as life gets more hectic and schedules get crazier, these are the people who seem to have it all together. Even when they're Just Like Us, pushing grocery carts or kids on swings, they have the glow of those who've got life figured out. And that's all us regular folk want. To have it under control. To appear perfect, if not actually be perfect.

Or maybe we've become so inundated with the images of outward perfection—photo spreads of Eva Longoria's shoe-lined closets, the impeccably dressed Beckham clan—that *People* readers everywhere think we're dropping the ball.

It's a chicken-or-the-egg issue. Do we obsess over celebrities because we want to be perfect? Or do we want to be perfect because we obsess over celebrities?

There's no way to be sure. Recent research has shown perfectionism to be an issue of genetics. One study found that identical twins are more similar than fraternal twins in terms of how much they idolize celebrity bodies, which would make this tendency more nature than nurture. But it can't all be hereditary, unless every woman I know—and plenty of men—shares this same gene. And perfectionism comes in degrees. Mine, I think, is fairly mild, and seems to emerge only when I'm comparing myself with other people. I don't need to make my bed with hospital corners (or at all), and I'm willing to be seen in public wearing a slightly wrinkled shirt. It's only when I see images of those who I deem "better" that I start to feel inadequate, as if I should really be a much-improved version of myself.

Other research finds that celebrities don't necessarily promote perfectionism, but instead help people build their own self-images. We create imagined relationships with stars to form the blueprint of who we want to be. Take Zara, a participant in a University of Arkansas, Fayetteville study on these relationships. According to the researchers: "Zara labeled different aspects of herself as 'goofball,' 'wanting to study,' 'positive,' and 'old-fashioned,' and she relied upon different celebrities—singer and *X Factor* judge Nicole Scherzinger (goofball); Emma Watson, 'Hermione' in the *Harry Potter* films (wanting to study); Victoria's Secret model Miranda Kerr (positive self); and Kate Middleton, Duchess of Cambridge (old-fashioned)—to execute and move between these various identities."

I do the same thing, and while these celebrities should be a source of inspiration, they often become a point of comparison instead. Once I've connected a part of my identity with a celebrity, I can't help but hold myself to that standard. You can label yourself as "positive like Miranda Kerr," but once you decide you must be *as* positive as Miranda Kerr, or *as* proper as Kate Middleton, you're demanding a lot.

The root of our perfectionism—the chicken or the egg—is hardly the point. These days, perfection and celebrity go hand in hand, whether we're talking about Jennifer or Martha Stewart or anyone in between. Magazines, twenty-four-hour entertainment channels, blogs, even the A-listers themselves, thrive on the celeb-perfection connection. Every day, pop culture sells us on the idea that both roads lead to happiness.

If I'm perfect, or at least more perfect, and if I live like the rich and famous, maybe I'll have complete life satisfaction.

Our rational sides reject this notion, but deep down we wonder. And we try our best to be a little bit more fabulous, just in case.

Or, at least, I certainly do.

* * *

Which brings me to this book.

Lately I've been feeling the opposite of perfect, or together, or A-list anything. As I write this, I'm unshowered in a sports bra, a ratty coral sweatshirt, and leggings that cut off at the calf (a big-time Tim Gunn no-no: *Leggings are not pants! Nothing should land mid-calf!*). I'd planned on working out but got caught up and no longer have time today. Caught up in writing, yes, but also reading recaps of *The Voice* and eavesdropping on the five-year-old at the café table next to me who just declared that 98 and 7 are her favorite numbers.

The amount of times I've made the internal and sweeping declaration that "Today will be different! I will finally get my life together!" is embarrassing, and it seems that every day I say it, my resolve somehow gets weaker. I splurge on a croissant, I switch on a DVR'd episode of *Parenthood* at noon, I leave the house, again, sans under-eye concealer.

Each small decision, alone, wouldn't be that big of a deal. But the choices build on themselves, one leading to the next, collectively causing me to feel completely off my game. So I have to wonder if the opposite is true. If opting to wear sweats and skip exercise can make an otherwise solid existence feel totally scattered, can wearing adorable jean shorts, gladiator sandals, aviator sunglasses, and a T-shirt with that just-right fit (see: every picture ever of Halle Berry at the grocery store) make me feel like everything's in check?

I've been toying with the idea of trying to imitate a celebrity for a while now. Not actually impersonating a star, or having plastic surgery to make me look like Jennifer or Angelina (Octomom, much?), but what if I did my research, reading about how these women work out, eat, sleep, dress, meditate, chase kids around to burn calories (because isn't that how they all claim to keep fit?), carve out time for family, and keep each pair of shoes in a clear plastic box with a picture on the outside for easy styling? And what if I actually did those things, too? Would I finally "get my life together," that nebulous concept that I figure, like porn, you know when you see it?

I'm not the first to consider emulating the celebrity good life in hopes of gaining higher life satisfaction. Take haircuts alone. Before there was The Rachel, there was The Farrah. And the most recent popular cut, The Blake Lively, is no different. "It's aspirational hair," one salon owner told *The New York Times.* "[Clients] don't just want the hair, they want the life."

There's research out there that says a manageable amount of celebrity adoration can actually be good for you. A 2008 study found that, in individuals with low self-esteem, merely thinking about a favorite celebrity could bring a confidence boost. "Because people form bonds in their mind with their favorite celebrities, they are able to assimilate the celebrity's characteristics in themselves and feel better about themselves when they think about that celebrity," Shira Gabriel, coauthor of the study, told *Time*. So if I think about Jennifer a lot, if I try to adopt some of her "characteristics"—wicked sense of humor! Yoga-induced calm! Tremendous legs!—I might feel like my own life is pulled together that much more. (You have to be careful though: Spiral too deep into the pit of tabloid obsession and you could find yourself plagued with Celebrity Worship Syndrome, downright addicted to gossip. It's a real condition: A celebaholic. Or something.)

The idea is that I'll stop flipping the pages of *InStyle* to see the fabulous and expensive clothes I can't afford, and use it instead as an inspiration manual. A regular vision board. Celebrity profiles could be lesson plans. I'll never have the means to buy a $3,000 handbag, but I can probably find an imitation. I can't hire a chef to whip me up a green smoothie, but I can throw some kale and ice in a blender.

In the pie of life, we each weigh the slices differently. Yes, I might put off work by checking out Jennifer's abs and mentally superimposing them onto my own, but I have friends who'd happily accept some extra belly flab if it meant they could throw the perfect dinner party or land on someone's—anyone's—best-dressed list.

We each have our hang-ups, but my parents taught me I could have it all. I'm pretty sure the "all" they were referring to consisted of family, career, and personal life, but as I grew up, inundated equally with messages from the women's movement and celebrity culture, my "all" became even more encompassing. It's the blessing and curse of my generation. We believe we can have it all, and are willing to work for it, but "all" is the family, the career, the personal life, the body, the clothes, the poise. We don't just want to conquer the world, we want to look amazing while doing it.

So I'm going to try. I'll tackle my life one celebrity at a time. Starting, of course, with Jennifer's body. If I adopt her fitness and diet routine as my own, maybe I can achieve her fresh-faced forever-young irresistible look. I'll take on Gwyneth Paltrow's kitchen, Sarah Jessica Parker's style, and Tina Fey's work ethic. I'll try the Garner-Affleck marriage on for size (their matching Red Sox hats have always made me wonder: Does the couple that watches sports together stay together?), and imitate Julia Roberts's serenity. To cap it all off, I'll emulate Beyoncé's, um, *everything*.

Eventually, I'll have collected my very own guidelines for living the good life. A meditation from Julia here, a joke from Tina there.

I can think of worse ways to live.

If I do all these things, if I use everything at my disposal to at least imitate the lifestyles of the rich and famous, will I, too, give off that glow of the have-it-all-together? And if I appear together, will I actually, suddenly, *feel* together?

In other words, if I appear perfect, will I feel perfect? And will I be a happier person for it?

That's what I'm determined to find out.

Jennifer, Gwyneth & Me

CHAPTER ONE

JENNIFER ANISTON'S BODY

"My advice: just stop eating shit every day."
                                        —Harper's Bazaar UK

"I work out almost every day, at least five or six days a week."   —InStyle

"I've said it so many times: I'm going to have children. I just know it."   —Vogue

The simple act of preparing to be Jennifer Aniston is hard work. Before I dive into my research, I make a list of the words I associate with everyone's favorite superstar. It reads as follows:

> *Funny*
>
> *Legs*
>
> *Yoga*
>
> *Forties*
>
> *Running*

Not so impressive.

I need to ramp up my knowledge before diving into my new lifestyle, so for the next twenty-four hours I pore over Jen-related research. *GQ, Vogue, Vanity Fair, Entertainment Weekly, Rolling Stone, Architectural Digest, Elle, InStyle, Fitness, People, Marie Claire, Self, Esquire, Good Housekeeping.* With these magazines and more, plus TV and radio interviews, I read about fifty profiles and watch or listen to nearly twenty clips.

Ground rules have been set: I'll only accept as truth the words that have come out of Jen's mouth. Despite tabloid rumors that she has tested all-cucumber or baby-food-only diets, I won't be incorporating those into my meal plan. I also won't be spending $20,000 on new lighting in my home because 1) that's insane and 2) just because *Us Weekly* reported it doesn't mean it's true.

Exceptions to the horse's-mouth rule will be quotes from Jen-approved sources. Her trainer Mandy Ingber. Her private chefs, Jill and Jewels Elmore. Her bestie, Courteney Cox. Jen has publicly confirmed these relationships, so I figure they've got no reason to lie.

After this daylong Aniston deep dive, my overall sense of the star, of what it takes to assume her level of fabulousness, is more well rounded. If you read enough profiles, you get to know a person. Or, I should say, you think you do. If the writer does his job, you begin to understand the subject's personality. Her demeanor. Her clothes. Her habits.

I've learned that Jen curses a lot, that she wears black more than any other color but considers herself a T-shirt-and-jeans kind of girl. She eats well and works out a ton (duh), though she doesn't seem anxious to give in to America's incessant hunger for every detail of her regimen. She seems tough. Not mean, but not warm-and-fuzzy, either. Guarded, independent, strong. She's able to both laugh at herself and stand up for herself. I feel as if we could be friends, but also that Jen might have little patience for me. She seems confident and self-assured, and she might not be smitten with a pal who's working so desperately to find nirvana that she's resorted to simply copying other people, no matter how well intentioned that copying may be.

The recurring theme in each article, be it from 1996 or 2013, is that Jen is America's BFF, the girl next door, the relatable one. This image really exploded in 2005, when she and husband Brad Pitt split up. Suddenly Jennifer was the woman scorned, and Team Aniston worked its way into common vernacular.

We identified with her because she, like so many of us, got hurt by a man. We idolized her because she became an even better—funnier, hotter, more confident—version of herself in the face of that hurt. And now we cheer for her as she lives out her fairy-tale ending—the handsome new fiancé, the blinding engagement ring, the happier-than-ever glow.

The reality of the Jennifer Aniston story is unclear—we'll never know how much of the whole love-triangle saga is true and how much of the narrative was created by the media—but we've adopted it as truth, and we follow it as if we're attending to the dramas of our very closest pal.

Other nuggets from an education in Aniston: She believes in the power of girlfriends (as opposed to her supposed rival, Angelina Jolie, who has said repeatedly that she doesn't have female friends), she smoked (but quit recently), she's totally fine with seminude photos (with a bod like that, who can blame her?), and she loves Mexican food and dirty martinis, though probably not together. There are some New Age hippie undertones to many of her musings, but just enough to make her sound laid-back and peaceful rather than kooky.

By the end of the day I'm excited to embark on this new lifestyle. If the photos from a 2008 *Vogue* article tell us anything, it's that Jennifer hit her peak at 40. I'm 30, and reading these profiles has me extra excited about the ten years ahead. Of being 43, she once told the *CBS Morning Show:* "I feel like I'm 30. I honestly didn't start to feel my best until I was in my 30s. Physically, I started eating better and taking better care of my body." And even though it's the kind of stock sound bite you might hear from any "aging" Hollywood actress, I believe it. Despite all the money, power, and fame Jen has that I never will, her words make me feel like I, too, might be heading into my best decade.

This strange combination—A-list mega-star who still feels totally relatable—is the most interesting thing about Jen. Dreamworks CEO Stacey Snider said it best in that *Vogue* story: "She's special enough to be somewhat unattainable but real enough that you can imagine a friendship, which is why you pursue her. . . . There's something so pretty and sunny and winning about her. You bask in the reflection of her goldenness."

An admission: This day spent researching—"Celebrity Eve" you might call it—could also be called my "Farewell to Food." When I concocted the idea of trying to live like a celebrity, it sounded fun and glamorous. Now that I have a better sense of what it means to get Jennifer Aniston's shape, I'm not so sure that "fun" is the word I'd use to describe it. I have days of dieting and working out ahead of me. Until then, I want to be sure I've tasted everything that Jennifer Aniston perhaps never has. A sticky bun for breakfast, a tomato and mozzarella with pesto sandwich for lunch (full fat dairy!), Chinese food (sesame chicken and veggie moo shu) for dinner, cupcake for dessert. It feels a bit like the night before the contestants go on *The Biggest Loser,* knowing that months of salmon and kale lie ahead. It also sort of grosses me out, and gives me the extra boost I need to dive into this endeavor.

With my final calorie binge behind me, I'm ready to chase the Jennifer Aniston lifestyle, specifically her hot body. If my goal for this project is to improve my overall existence—to go from unstruc-

tured scatterbrain to in-control, confident, happy, life-conquerer—
I should start with my most basic possession, my physical self. It's
not just about having Jennifer's lean legs and cut arms (though I'll
take two of each, please), it's also about feeling healthy. Part of the
reason I've had trouble living the life I want lately is because I
haven't had the energy, so I'm ready to make some changes.

Let me explain. Nine months ago, I lost my job. I worked at
the website for a TV show that went off the air, and a large majority of my department got the boot. The layoffs weren't a surprise,
since we knew the show was ending, so I had planned for my of-
ficeless future. Or so I thought.

Careerwise, my preparation paid off. I knew I wanted to pursue full-time writing when the job was over, so I had started making contacts, pitching stories, and getting assignments. By the
time I lost my steady paycheck, I felt confident that some money
would roll in, and that I might actually be able to make a living
out of doing what I love.

But I didn't plan for the lack of routine. For the past eight
years I got up at the same time, went into an office, and planned
errands and workouts and dates with friends around the forty-
hour workweek. When that lifestyle changed, I was pretty excited.
Working out during the day! No more battling weekend crowds
for groceries! Daily productivity . . . in pajamas!

As it turns out, the whole work-from-home thing is a blessing
and a curse. On the days when I get up on time, put on jeans, and
go to the coffee shop near my apartment, it's an incredible gift.
On the days when I snooze two hours past my alarm, forget to
turn the lights on until 4 P.M., and don't get around to showering, it's, well, less than incredible. That's when I feel like a mess,
like someone paralyzed by a lack of structure, someone who can't
get anything done.

A few years ago, before I got married, I was the queen of routine. I woke up at 6:30 every morning, grabbed my exercise clothes and bagged lunch, and drove to the gym. I ran for forty-five minutes, usually five miles, and did sixty push-ups before heading to work. I spent my days in the office, and evenings with my husband, Matt, or friends or *Law & Order: SVU*. The repetitive nature of my life could be boring, for sure, but I rarely felt adrift. Then Matt and I got married and those five workouts a week turned into two or three, if that. When I became my own boss, I had just as much work to do, but a harder time getting myself in front of a desk to actually do it. A set schedule went by the wayside. The flexibility of my new lifestyle, complete with the ability to sleep through an alarm or work in my sweats, reinforced a general lethargy that affected my every day.

Which is how I ended up here.

Nine months later I feel like I'm constantly playing catch-up—my day should have started earlier, my house should be cleaner, my inbox should be more organized, and my meals should be less processed.

I know what you're thinking: *You have a husband you love, a career you always wanted, you're healthy and you're happy and you're complaining about . . . oversleeping? High-class problems.*

But I'm not alone. In her book *Be Happy Without Being Perfect: How to Break Free from the Perfection Deception,* Dr. Alice Domar writes about the pressure women put on themselves to get everything right. "Whether or not we work outside the home, we hear little voices—from ourselves, from society—reminding us of what we 'should' be. From the minute we drag ourselves out of bed in the morning till the minute we fall asleep at night, we are inundated with messages that tell us we should be thin, beautiful, successful, and sexy while being exceptional parents, supportive spouses, superlative employees, and cheerful volunteers. Oh, and we're supposed to get restaurant-quality Thanksgiving dinner for twenty-three people on the table without breaking a sweat. So, despite all the progress we've made, perfectionism is holding us back."

Compared to some of Dr. Domar's more extreme patients—women who feel like failures because they keep a cluttered closet or order too much takeout—my own perfectionist tendencies are pretty lax. I don't yet have kids to feel guilty about leaving with a sitter and I can always go to bed no matter how many dishes are in the sink (just ask my husband). I'll never offer to host Thanksgiving and I don't mind asking for help when I need it. But I'm someone who dreams of a life where everything has its place. I'd like to cross an errand off my to-do list, and make my bed, and cook for my husband, and run five miles, and chat on the phone with long-distance friends, and see local friends, and meditate, and drink forty-eight fluid ounces of water, and write at least one thousand words, and read forty pages, and get eight hours of sleep . . . Every. Single. Day.

I'm no therapist, so I don't know if these desires qualify me as a "normal" perfectionist ("striving for reasonable and realistic standards that leads to a sense of self-satisfaction and enhanced self-esteem") or a "neurotic" one ("a tendency to strive for excessively high standards . . . motivated by fears of failure and concern about disappointing others"). Probably somewhere in between. I doubt the standards I strive for are always reasonable or realistic, but I'm not afraid of failing at said goals, either. I've failed at them plenty—never have I come close to crossing off all the items on my wish list—and I've gotten by. Dr. Domar warns that perfectionism is bad for a woman's mental state. We are constantly striving for the impossible, falling short, and beating ourselves up about it, she says. Research backs her up. One 2007 study found that perfectionists are at a greater risk for mental distress, and that the condition is often at the root of issues like depression and addiction. But the reason I want to tackle all the items on that laundry list—the cooking and the running and the reading—is because I really do believe it will make me happy. I picture myself going to sleep in a previously unknown state of Zen, in which I can rest easy knowing I've done everything I set out to do. Research says otherwise, but sometimes I can't shake the feeling that checkmarks on the to-do list pave the road to happiness.

My emotional self is clearly at odds with my rational self, the one that buys into science and studies. But here's what I do know: I'm in the company of millions of women across the country, all of whom are trying to get a firm grasp on every moving part in the orbit of their lives.

Before I even launch my pursuit to live Jennifer's life, I'm faced with one minor catch. I don't have Jennifer's money. She has a personal trainer, private chef, hairstylist, and probably a wardrobe stylist, too. I canceled my gym membership when I lost my job and cook about once a month, instead opting for frozen Trader Joe's meals that I tell my mother-in-law I "prepare."

To be Jennifer Aniston you need access to a gym. The one near my apartment—with the hardest classes in Chicago and trainers who already have Jen-caliber bodies—costs $195 a month. And so, after trying out a class a few weeks back, I approached the front desk.

"Do you guys have any plans to do a Groupon?" I asked the studio's owner.

"We don't," she said. We had chatted when I first signed up, so she knew my employment situation. "You were just laid off, right?"

"Yup. Which means I have plenty of time to work out," I said. "But less money to work out with."

She smiled a that-sucks-but-there's-nothing-I-can-do smile.

"Maybe you need someone to work the front desk?" I asked.

"You want desk hours? Could you watch kids?" She nodded to the Kids Club, the studio's version of child care.

"Um, sure," I said. I was a babysitter once. Fifteen years ago, but no matter. I'm 30. I can watch a kid or two for an hour. "Would I get discounted classes?"

She told me the job paid $12 an hour plus a free membership.

And that's how I ended up, just last week, fielding a four-year-old's request to wipe his poop.

As gym babysitter, I've had up to nine kids in my care at once, with ages ranging anywhere from six weeks to ten years. But last week there were only three of us: Me, four-year-old Charlie, and six-year-old Sam. We spent the majority of the hour playing Wii. Until Charlie needed to use the bathroom.

"Okay, I'll take you," I said.

Five minutes later he was still in there.

"Charlie? Everything okay?" I asked.

"Yup. I'm done."

"Okay, then clean up and come on out," I said.

Three more minutes passed. Nothing.

"Charlie? You good?"

"Yup, I'm done," he said.

"Do you know how to wipe and come out?"

"Yes."

Another three minutes.

"Charlie?"

"I need help," he said. "Can you wipe my poop?"

I'm not particularly interested in touching a small child's behind until I have one of my own. But that wasn't my only concern. For starters, how much help is appropriate when you're an adult with a small boy you've just met? I'm just trying to get free gym classes here. I've seen enough very special episodes of *Diff'rent Strokes* to know that you've got to be careful when touching small children.

This would never happen to Jennifer.

In the end I went to the owner, who has three kids herself, and she took over wiping duties. "If kids ever need help in the bathroom, feel free," she tells me. "You're okay to wipe."

Yippee.

So now I have a gym membership. I also have access to Jennifer's personal yoga instructor and private chefs. As it turns out, being the "personal" anything to Jennifer Aniston is a direct route to fame and fortune. Or at least press and publication. Yoga instructor Mandy Ingber became one of Hollywood's most coveted celebrity trainers after she and Jennifer did a spread together for *Self* magazine. These days she's all over the fitness magazines, talking about how great Jen is at tree pose, or how she grunts in plank. I downloaded Ingber's "Yogalosophy" DVD, which includes a 26-second intro from Ms. Aniston herself, for only $14.95. That's cheaper than a single drop-in class at my usual yoga spot, so I feel good about it. Celebrity access on a budget will hopefully be a recurring theme this year.

Like Ingber, sisters Jill and Jewels Elmore used their connection to Jen to build a brand. And like Yogalosophy, their first cookbook, *The Family Chef,* includes an Aniston intro. Before she met Jewels and Jill, Jen writes, her diet consisted of "prepackaged Zone meals, overcooked takeout and scrounging for the occasional piece of cheese." Her private chefs taught her "how to nourish [her] body with real food—food that's truly and naturally life sustaining and delicious." I can't exactly hire the Elmore sisters to fly out to Chicago and cook for me, so instead I shell out $25.15 for the cookbook. If I can't have Jen's chefs, at least I can have their recipes.

Armed with a yoga DVD, a cookbook, a zillion celebrity profiles, and a Google alert to let me know if any big Aniston-related news breaks, I'm basically a mini-Jen (or maxi-Jen, I guess, since I've probably got twenty-five pounds on her). I've even put together some guidelines, an easy reference sheet to keep track of how Ms. Aniston lives according to the woman herself.

- **Exercise:** Forty minutes of cardio five or six days a week—spinning, running, elliptical, or a combination of all three. Pilates one day a week. Yoga three days a week. Eight-pound weights for travel. (Jen does arm exercises during long phone calls or TV watching.)
- **Diet:** Fish, quinoa, lentils, and green vegetables. Coffee, dairy, wine, dirty martinis. Four sport bottles of SmartWater a day. Diet Coke. Omega Cure liquid fish oil and resveratrol. Avoid fried food for the most part. Indulgence: Mexican food.
- **Fashion:** Go-to classy: Jeans, a great wedge, a beautiful blouse, and a blazer. Go-to casual: Comfy pants, flip-flops, T-shirt. Colors: black, nude, gray/silver.

So there it is. The Jennifer Aniston Manual, as evidenced by my research. I'll probably lean into the lifestyle—working out six days a week, often twice a day, is something I'll have to work up to. It's a time-consuming endeavor. You have more free hours to exercise when looking good is your job, but I still have to do the whole making-a-living thing during the day, so I'll do my best. Same with the food and water. Hydration is a big problem for me—I meet my daily liquid quota with Diet Coke, a fact I'm not proud of. I'm glad to read that Jennifer is a bit of an addict, too— "It's the monkey on my back," she has said—so I don't have to give up soda, but water would be a good addition.

Overall, I've developed three Aniston mantras as I embark on my quest: Get moving every day. When in doubt, wear a neutral. And, my personal favorite, as told to *Harper's Bazaar UK*, don't eat shit.

* * *

Day one of Project Aniston starts with good intentions. I set my alarm for 6 A.M., about two hours earlier than I normally wake (the benefits of not having to get ready for the office). Jennifer once told Oprah that she starts her day before dawn. "I wake up and go, 'The sun's coming up soon and that means I get to have a cup of coffee and read the paper,'" she said. This sounds like a lovely way to start the day. Much better than my own rising routine, which involves reaching for my iPhone while I'm still half asleep and checking email in bed because the East Coast is already at work. Then I race to my computer to write a blog post or answer a question from an editor, forgoing the normal person's easing-into-the-day routine. There is no relaxed cup of coffee while watching the sunrise. No kicking back while I read the paper. There is only an eventual two-minute walk to the grocery store, hair unwashed, where I pick up a 20-ounce soda to drink while back at the computer.

Even before I started studying Jennifer, I knew I felt best on the days I woke up early. If I'm up by 7, I'm actually ready to face the world by 9.

Today, however, is not that day. When the alarm goes off, Matt gives me a little shove. He's sleeping in this morning—my lawyer husband usually gets to the office long before I even wake up—so my decision to set the alarm for two hours earlier than normal doesn't excite him.

"What's going on?" he mumbles. "Do you have a deadline?" A past-due assignment is usually the only thing that gets me up with the sun.

"Hmmmppphh," I grunt, slamming the alarm quiet and going back to sleep. This continues every nine minutes for the next twenty-seven, until I finally reset the alarm for 8:30.

Granted, I didn't go to bed at 10, which would be necessary to get Jennifer's "at least eight hours of sleep a night" and still wake up as planned. But succeeding at day one, task one, would have been nice.

"What was that about?" Matt asks when I stumble into the bathroom as he's finishing his morning shave.

"Jennifer Aniston gets up before sunrise," I say.

He nods, but I can see his eye roll reflected in the mirror.

Oh, Matt. He is my biggest supporter, and he'd probably tell you my life is pretty great as is. He's never suggested I need any sort of physical overhaul, or that I should work harder or dress more glamorously. I know he wouldn't mind if I held up my end in his pursuit to keep our house clean (he is the neat freak, I am the mess), or if I could fall asleep without turning the TV on after he's already passed out, but he's never implied that I was anything less than fabulous. When I complain about feeling gross or being unhappy with my day-to-day, he tells me I look great, that my career is on track, and that he wouldn't want me to change a thing. If *I* want me to change, he says, then I should go for it. But not on his account.

My husband doesn't need any help in the get-your-life-in-check category. I've honestly never, not once, seen him feel overwhelmed or stressed. His ability to maintain perspective in any circumstance is one of his greatest sources of pride. And my biggest source of annoyance. If something doesn't go his way, he shrugs it off. Or, in extreme cases, he curses, lets out a quick cathartic scream, and moves on. (This really only happens each time he loses another pair of sunglasses.) Matt has a self-confidence I've never known, so he gets a kick out of my neverending self-improvement projects.

Matt and I represent the typical male-female breakdown when it comes to perfectionism. According to a 2009 study, more women than men feel inadequate when it comes to meeting the standards they set for themselves at home and at work. In the office, 38 percent of women felt they didn't meet their own standards, compared with 24 percent of men. When it came to home and family life, 30 percent of women felt they'd fallen short, compared to only 17 percent of men. But my husband is on board with this project. Its effect on him will be minimal and positive: namely, more home-cooked meals and a less frazzled wife.

On this first day, I take a 3 P.M. break from the article that's due tomorrow morning to do some yoga. The Mandy Ingber download came with one thirty-minute routine, plus five bonus tracks.

Eventually I'm supposed to do two at a time—the half-hour, plus one bonus—but since this is my first attempt at her workout, and I don't know what to expect in terms of difficulty, and I'm short on time (tomorrow I *will* wake up early!), I opt for the thirty minutes only.

Mandy Ingber is peppy. She's not your average Zen instructor who pretends the only acceptable yoga motivation is serenity and centering. Instead, she acknowledges that I'm just as likely to be on the mat to improve my bikini body as I am to improve my mind. Five minutes in, she advises that many yogis use a mantra to remember their intention while on the mat. "I'll share my mantra in a moment," she says.

Cut to Mandy, three minutes later, pulsing in a standing lunge. "I have a great ass, I have a great ass, I have a great ass." She giggles. "That's my mantra!"

I appreciate that she doesn't take herself too seriously.

She's right, though. She has a great ass. And great arms, abs, and legs. She looks like a lean, muscular mini-human. I want to put her in my pocket.

Halfway through the workout Mandy talks about her obsession with firming her inner thighs. "Maybe it's because when I was younger all the magazines said you looked best if your thighs didn't touch," she says.

Apparently perfectionist messages miss no one.

The workout is half yoga, half toning exercises, like the Jane Fonda–esque dog-at-a-fire-hydrant leg lifts. It's not easy. I've been doing yoga (with varying degrees of regularity) for about ten years, and while the moves are fairly basic, there is a lot of lunging and pulsing and painful muscle burning. I assume that Jen's yoga workout is a variation of this, but probably for ninety minutes instead of thirty. Plus a separate cardio session. Still, even this quick burst gives me the endorphin boost I need to stare down my deadline.

Amazingly, succeeding at this one little task of living-room yoga motivates me for my next Aniston-related activity: grocery shopping. At present, I don't cook much, but I've decided to start my celebrity-approved meal plan with the salmon Jennifer extols in *The Family Chef*. The recipe is titled "Fancy Restaurant-Style Salmon with Maitake Mushrooms." It looks pretty schmancy, but is actually just seared salmon seasoned with salt, pepper, and lemon zest with a side of asparagus and a mushroom-shallot mixture. I'm not able to find maitake mushrooms at my local store—I probably wouldn't recognize them if I did—so I grab oyster mushrooms instead. I have no idea if this is the right substitute, but the instructions indicate there should be mushroom "petals," which the oyster variety seem to have.

Good enough for me.

On the walk home, my phone rings.

"Have you gone to the grocery store yet?" I already surprised Matt with the big news that I'm cooking salmon tonight.

"I have."

"Oh, I was going to ask if you could include some sort of vegetable but never mind," he says. Apparently, my reputation for serving a piece of protein alone on a plate with no side dish precedes me.

"I got asparagus," I say. "And mushrooms."

"Wow!" There is genuine shock and enthusiasm in Matt's voice.

This is embarrassing.

———

At 7:18 I start making dinner. "Ooh, classy," Matt says as he walks by and sees me tying a long chive around each bundle of asparagus. This is already a step in the right direction. In the past, the cookbooks I've used most are *The Healthy College Cookbook* (yes, I'm 30), *The Biggest Loser Cookbook,* and the *Weight Watchers* cookbooks. Not that these options aren't worthy, but they don't exactly emphasize presentation. They're about calories and easy prep, not securing asparagus with a knotted chive.

Dinner is ready at 7:58. According to the directions, this recipe takes only "moments to prepare." For me, forty minutes is pretty good. If you haven't already gathered, I'm not exactly a whiz in the kitchen.

I'm excited about this venture. I have a plate with a healthy fish and two different kinds of vegetables. I actually believe this is a meal that Jennifer might eat—the lack of carbs certainly says so. And it tastes good. It's filling, and the salmon has a golden crisp to it, a sign that I might have cooked fish correctly for the first time in my life. The oyster mushrooms are, well, *meh,* if you ask me, but Matt likes them so much that when he spots the leftovers on my plate he shoves a fistful in his mouth.

Success.

I go to bed on day one with mixed feelings. I did yoga and cooked a private chef-style dinner, which is certainly a good start. But I overslept, and because of that I didn't take time to put on a cute outfit in which to face the day. I drank more water than usual, though certainly not four bottles. And despite the dinner, the rest of my eating was just okay. (Does Jennifer ever have a Twizzler binge?)

My life doesn't feel more in control after day one. I don't feel like I have it all figured out. In fact, I just feel more aware of what *isn't* in control. All the not-perfects shine a bit brighter. But there's a lesson lurking here. I got a disproportionate amount of satisfaction from indulging in something as small as a half-hour daytime yoga break or cooking a nice meal. Doing a few things "right" gave me a sense of accomplishment that day. I've always been a "do it all, do it right, or do nothing" kind of gal. One handful of chips means I should eat the whole bag because healthy eating is shot anyway. A missed workout means I should stay on the couch because today will be lazy all around. That kind of thing. Today I checked off a couple of the tasks I set out to do, and at least it feels better than yesterday.

The next day, I make some morning adjustments. Getting up before sunrise seems like a task to work up to, so I set my alarm for 7:02. Turns out, though, that I don't need an alarm at all, since Matt comes bounding into our room at 6:45 screaming, "WWJD! WWJD! Time to get up! Time to live fabulously!"

I want to punch him.

Matt isn't one to take on a self-improvement project himself, but he's happy to cheer me on, especially if there's something in it for him.

"Which celebrity keeps a superclean house?" he asked me when I told him of my plan.

"Martha Stewart, I guess."

"Great! When do you get to her?"

"I don't," I told him. "Most of my celebrities have maids, I assume."

He has chosen to ignore this, and tells anyone who asks about my quest that he can't wait to meet his wife, Martha.

––––––––

By 10 A.M., I've run forty minutes, done thirty-five minutes of yoga, and eaten a homemade egg-white omelet with part-skim mozzarella and leftover broccoli from the other night's sesame chicken. I decided on this meal by googling "what Jennifer Aniston eats for breakfast," because I figure I should be as literal as possible for the first few days before trusting myself to make any Jennifer-inspired decisions on my own.

Baby steps.

I shouldn't really need Jennifer Aniston to teach me this, but getting up early and fitting in a workout first thing gives the entire day a feeling of accomplishment. Knowing that if nothing else goes as planned I've at least done most of my Jen-mandated activities lifts the burden of fabulousness. I even take a quick break in the afternoon to run to the store and pick up celebrity Pilates instructor Mari Windsor's workout DVD. Now I have everything necessary to follow Jennifer's workout to a T. Being fabulous never seemed so easy.

The day feels totally in control—half a Greek salad for lunch, the other half saved for a 4 P.M. snack—until the evening, when I attend a work fund-raiser with Matt. The dinner options are pasta with tomato sauce and chicken, or pasta with cream sauce and broccoli. I'm pretty sure that pasta is the devil's food, at least according to the stars, but what's a famished girl who worked out twice as much as normal today to do?

I anticipate this being one of the biggest problems of my celebrity-caliber life. Socializing and eating only salmon and kale and quinoa are pretty much mutually exclusive, at least in my hometown of Chicago. Maybe not in L.A., where quinoa and brown lentils seem to be a staple at every salad bar, but even there I bet it gets tricky. And I don't want to foist my celebrity eating (or non-eating, as it could easily become) on friends by refusing to share a pizza at dinner or vetting the menu if they're hosting book club or a girls night. The friend with crazy dietary restrictions is never the fun one.

I know that celebrities go out to eat—*Us Weekly* tells me so!— but every time I imagine any of the inspirational (aspirational?) ladies on my list at The Ivy or some such trendy restaurant, I'm reminded of a profile I once read of celebrity stylist Rachel Zoe in *The New York Times*: "Zoe looked down at her plate. Steamed vegetables were fanned around a small dollop of sauce. 'What is this?' she asked. Zoe picked up her untouched plate and beckoned the waitress. 'I need to send this back,' she said. 'Bring it to me without the sauce, please.'" I want to feel together and fabulous and in control, but I don't want to be out in public acting entitled, sending back any plate with a drop of dressing. There's no faster way to lose that next dinner invitation. And ultimately, what will be more vital to my happiness? The pounds lost by cutting out sauce, or dinners with friends? I'm guessing the latter.

My sister-in-law has a theory that everyone has "five fun pounds." Anyone could lose the extra weight if she cut out restaurant meals, social gatherings with friends and family, and drinking, she says. But is that kind of lifestyle worth it?

At the end of my first week of Project Jennifer, Matt and I go out to dinner. I announce en route that I will be drinking a dirty martini, Jen's alcohol of choice. The restaurant, GT Fish & Oyster, seems like an appropriate celeb eating option. Lots of fish and seafood, obviously. The hiccup comes when the dessert menu lands on our table.

"I can't decide between the salted banana tart and the sticky toffee cake," I tell Matt after studying the options.

"WWJD," he says. Matt's a healthy eater. He'll indulge in dessert once in a while, but whenever I want, say, a French fry, he shoots me the eyes of judgment. Tonight he's not in the mood for dessert, and seems to have found an unexpected ally in my celebrity muse.

"One, she indulges sometimes," I say. "Two, you are the worst."

We skip dessert.

Week one was, overall, a success. I lost a pound and a half, worked out six days (including some two-a-days), and feel like I'm on the right track. The biggest surprise isn't how successful it was but how easy it felt. I expected lots of hunger and exhaustion and boredom. Not the case. I've been fairly full, energized, and entertained by my constant Jennifer research.

But I'm not naïve. I know this euphoria will be short-lived. When reality sets in—parties full of cupcakes, deadlines that turn two hours of exercise into a nagging chore rather than a luxury— I know this lifestyle will be harder, and so much less fun, to keep up. I just have to hope it'll feel worth it. Like when you realize your dreamy new boyfriend has a snoring problem. Those Friday night sleepovers are a little less exciting, but it's no reason to call them off altogether.

Over the next couple of weeks my Jennifer guidelines come in handy. I gave Matt a hard time, but the WWJD mantra has merit. My muse is perhaps a bit less sacred than the original J, but I'm taking what works for me and running with it. I've learned to actually get up with my alarm—assuming three snoozes still counts as getting up—and I'm making a routine of working out first thing, before launching into work. Dinners have consisted of walnut-encrusted whitefish, grilled halibut with red quinoa, and lentil soup. The only thing that could make these meals more Jen-like would be if Courteney Cox were dining alongside me.

I land a job interview at a local magazine on day 14. I'm not sure I want to give up the be-my-own-boss lifestyle, but this is a position I've been eyeing for years. At first, I have no idea what to wear. I haven't been on an interview since 2007 and those pants don't fit anymore. So I ask myself: What would Jennifer wear? I scroll through my mental Rolodex of paparazzi shots and the solution is clear. A black button-down shirt. It's her uniform. So I sift through my closet and find a black shirtdress. I throw on a beaded belt with a white, gold, and black pattern and voilà. It's the perfect choice: classy but not fancy, flattering but not showy.

A week later I learn I didn't get the job, but no matter. At least I looked good.

Of all the nuggets Jen has shared about her eating habits, her simple advice to "stop eating shit every day" haunts me most. Every time I reach for a snack, a mini-Aniston on my shoulder asks, "Is this shit?" It sounds silly, but it's as good a guiding dietary principle as I've ever had. Because "shit" doesn't necessarily mean something with a lot of fat or calories or carbs. It's open to my discretion, and I'm guessing "shit" applies to my go-to microwave meals, which are low-calorie but also low-nutrient, made with exactly zero whole food ingredients. The rule makes me second-guess my morning power bar, too, which I'm thinking might just be a gussied-up version of a candy bar.

Don't eat shit. When in doubt wear neutrals. Get moving every day.

Better rules to live by there never were.

* * *

Over the last few months, I have incorporated one ritual that hasn't come from Jennifer. The morning pee-on-a-stick.

Matt and I decided, about seven months ago, that we were ready to start trying for a baby. Or, I should say, Matt decided *he* was ready. Emotionally, I've been ready for as long as I can remember. I was never the girl who fantasized about her wedding. I didn't have my dress designed in my head when Matt proposed; I didn't care about the colors. I didn't even see the flowers until I arrived to walk down the aisle. Instead, I've always had baby fever. I wave and make faces at little ones in restaurants, even as others roll their eyes at the inevitable screaming that will disrupt their meal. I cry at every Hollywood birth scene. (*Father of the Bride Part II*? Major tearjerker.) When I moved to Chicago and my married friends said, "Let's make a no-baby pact! We'll wait until we're thirty-five!" I made no such guarantees. Instead, I stared in awe at the pregnant bellies that seemed to flood the streets of my Lincoln Park neighborhood and imagined my own one-day nursery when I was supposed to be shopping for friends' babies instead. On the night of my bridal shower, after celebrating with my pregnant sister-in-law, I dreamt not about my nuptials but of the offspring that would hopefully come as a result.

People have always been surprised that I'm so baby-crazed. Apparently I don't come off as warm and fuzzy in that goo-goo-ga-ga kind of way. When my former roommate saw how giddy I got around infants, she looked at me with total confusion. "You can't like babies," she said. "You don't even like dogs!"

Theoretically, I've wanted a child for ages. Practically speaking, however, I knew Matt and I weren't ready until a little over a year ago. We enjoyed quiet Sunday mornings too much. We got exhausted watching our two-year-old nephew for an hour. We had travel plans and work plans that we both agreed were pre-baby endeavors.

For me, the logistical ready-for-baby decision came gradually. First, I found myself more jealous than enamored when I saw moms with their BabyBjörns or dads pushing strollers. Then I noticed I'd stopped dreaming up potential exotic vacations and instead cushioned every future plan in my head with "unless I'm pregnant." I forgot to take my birth control pill for a day or two, and rather than seeing it as a sign of my absentmindedness, I saw it as an opportunity. The idea of having a family suddenly seemed more exciting than any of those quiet Sunday mornings.

I broached the subject with Matt at dinner one night.

"So, are we ready to, um, maybe, have a baby?" I asked over a spicy tuna roll.

Matt let out his nervous, oh-I-guess-we're-talking-about-this laugh. "Well, I don't really picture myself being a father," he said.

Hold up.

"Excuse me?" I asked. Babies are something we've both always agreed upon. This was nonnegotiable.

"Of course I want kids one day," he said. "But I don't think I'll ever wake up and say, 'Today, I'm ready.'"

But that's exactly what happened to me, I told Matt. I didn't want him to feel pressured, but I did need him to know this was something I wanted. Preferably sooner than later.

Still, we had to be in agreement. And so we waited.

Matt knew the decision was on him. I longed to add to our brood, to have a little bugger that was part my husband and part me. But I needed Matt to feel that way, too. A family isn't something I wanted to create under threat or ultimatum or nagging. We both had to want it.

And then, one day, a couple of months after telling me he couldn't envision fatherhood, Matt said he was ready.

I never asked him what changed his mind. One thing I learned about my husband long ago is that he needs time to make decisions, especially the really big ones. But once he commits to something, he sticks to it, and believes in it.

And so, the trying began.

Back then, my understanding of "trying" (a phrase I've never especially liked, too visual) was that man and wife decide they're ready for parenthood and commence with some fanfare. In reality, I had no idea what the practice entailed. Sex, sure. But there had to be more to it. Otherwise "trying" would just be "doing."

There's a reason I was so in the dark about baby-making: No one talks about it. Of course I learned the basics once upon a time in a conversation with my parents that, luckily, I barely remember. And I put a condom on a banana in seventh grade Sex Ed. But the world of ovulation tracking, basal-temperature taking, and sex planning? New to me. Most of my friends are non-moms, and if some of them are working on babies, we haven't discussed it. We usually talk about everything—I could recite to you one friend's bowel-moving schedule if it came to that—but the intricacies of planning a family seem strictly off-limits.

The reason for this, or so I've gathered from bits and pieces of conversation I've squeezed out of anyone willing to go there, is that no woman wants to set herself up to admit she's struggling to conceive. Talk about perfectionism. We're so afraid of "failing" at what seems so easy for irresponsible teenagers that we banish the topic from conversation. No matter that the supposed failure is completely out of our control.

Before the phrase "basal temperature" was even in my vocabulary, I talked about baby-making plenty. Until six months ago, I often told friends I was convinced I was infertile—to quote Marnie from *Girls,* "I've been sexually irresponsible enough in my life thus far that I should've gotten pregnant by now, and I never have." But now that I've been trying, unsuccessfully, to get pregnant, I'm scared to bring it up. I don't want to admit failure, or have others judge me, or speak worries aloud only for them to come true.

I've never been a believer in *The Secret,* but now seems no time to test it.

In the seven months since we started trying, I've had one brief moment where I thought I might be pregnant. I was nearly a week late, but after several negative tests, I realized that what I thought was a missed period was actually just a body on a completely irregular clock.

Which brings me to these pee sticks, or, more scientifically, ovulation predictor kits. During my first month using these digital tests, a big fat empty circle greeted me for three straight weeks. That was the "closed for business" sign, an indicator that I wasn't yet ovulating. Seeing it every day for twenty-one days was a major source of frustration, since it meant my body wasn't working on the fourteen-day schedule I thought all female forms adhered to. The first day I got the smiley face—telling me the fertility window was finally open—was exciting. Way exciting. I was giddy, probably like most "trying" women when they learn they're actually pregnant. I was thrilled just to be ovulating. At least the machine was working.

There hasn't been much luck since then. Smiley faces, yes, but no babies.

It's been a long seven months.

Simultaneously pursuing pregnancy and the perfect body is coun-
terintuitive. As is pursuing pregnancy and any kind of perfect,
pulled-together existence. In both cases, the end goals don't exactly mesh. If the perfect body includes flat abs and perky boobs,
and being pulled together means no spit-up on your shirt, then
becoming a mother runs counter to my current plan. But that's
part of the reason this quest appeals to me so much. I want to get
my life in the best shape possible before a baby comes in and turns
it upside down. Not unlike how I've always planned to get nice
and chunky before heading to the island when I compete on *Survivor*. A girl needs to think ahead.

On the other hand, a life inspired by celebrity worship probably should involve a baby bump, or at least some hearty speculation. It's the moneymaker when it comes to newsstand sales.
Snooki, Jessica Simpson, Beyoncé—the bigger their stomachs, the
higher the tabloid-photo price tag. *People* magazine has an entire
website devoted to celebrity babies. Jenny Schafer, a senior editor
for CelebrityBabyScoop.com, once told CNN that the obsession
with celebrity offspring boils down to relatability. "People want to
see if celebs are really like us," she said. "Do their children have
temper tantrums in public? Do their children use soothers? Do
they ever get frustrated in public with their kids?"

In the realm of tabloid baby speculation, Jennifer is, again, the
reigning queen. A slideshow on Celebuzz.com highlights a whop-
ping twenty-one magazine covers claiming that she's pregnant.
Twins with John Mayer! Adopting from Mexico! Pregnant at 40!
Fertility Treatment! Justin Theroux Touched Her Stomach, She
Must Be Carrying Triplets!

Jen squashed one round of rumors when she spoke to Britain's

Hello! magazine in 2011. "No, we're not pregnant," she said, referencing her then-boyfriend Theroux. "It's just I quit smoking, so I've gained a couple of pounds."

Can you imagine having to explain that, no, you're not expecting, you've just packed on a few LBs . . . especially if you look like Jennifer Aniston?

This could be another reason women keep their pregnancy plans, or hopes, a secret. The more that people know you're trying, the more they dissect your every sip of alcohol, loose-fitting shirt, or extra pudge. No one wants to be the tabloid headline of her local rumor mill, subject to speculation of whether she's pregnant or just plain fat.

So I haven't told many people about my baby chase. My mom, my closest friends, that's about it. And today, I'm one day late. I don't feel any different, and I'm pretty sure I know what the results will be, but I decide to take a pregnancy test anyway. No matter how realistic and prepared-for-the-worst I try to be, each month I have a bit of hope. For the three minutes I have to wait, I get a flutter of nervous excitement in my stomach.

Jennifer has consistently confirmed she wants kids, eventually. That we have in common. As I check the result of my test, I learn another commonality: It looks like now is not the time for either of us.

* * *

I've been doing my yoga workouts almost daily. My butt's getting firmer and higher. Mandy Ingber and I are basically best friends, even if she doesn't know it yet. I feel that way about Jennifer, too, which is mildly embarrassing. I joke about it with friends—"Oh, Jen told me to eat it," I'll say when extolling the virtues of kale—

but this sort of celebrity relationship is a real scientific phenomenon. It's called a parasocial interaction, a term coined by sociologists Donald Horton and Richard R. Wohl in the 1950s. A parasocial interaction is a one-sided relationship where one party knows a lot about the second party, but the second party knows nothing, or next to nothing, about the first. It is most commonly observed between celebrities and their followers, which shouldn't come as a shock. After all, magazines rake in big money by making fans feel like they know a star intimately. And I'm not alone when it comes to my first choice of parasocial pal. According to one expert, the cast of my favorite sitcom is more prone to parasocial relationships than most. "Many people have probably spent more time with the characters on *Friends* than they have with most of their real-life friends," Kansas State University cognitive psychologist Richard Harris has said on the topic of these imaginary friendships. "Of course they haven't interacted with them—it's very one-sided. People can, if drama is particularly well acted and written, identify with the characters. That's a significant relationship." Perhaps this is why my aunt and I sometimes email each other just to say how much we miss our Friends.

Journalist Jake Halpern, author of *Fame Junkies: The Hidden Truth Behind America's Favorite Addiction,* which investigates our cultural obsession with the rich and famous, admitted on NPR's *All Things Considered* that he too found himself in a parasocial relationship. His was with the characters on *Cheers.* "At times, Norm, Cliff, Carla and Sam have formed, well, kind of a parasocial family to which I yearn to belong. I suppose as hideously hackneyed as it sounds, it's just like the show's theme song goes. Sometimes you want to go where everybody knows your name, and they're always glad you came. Only they don't know your name, and they really don't even know you came."

What makes these relationships even trickier, especially in the age of social media, is that it sometimes feels as if certain celebrities *do* know you came. Interactions on Twitter, for example, increasingly blur the line of accessibility. A superfan tweets at, say, Jessica Alba, and she responds. Suddenly it seems that you two actually know each other, that you might as well call each other at home. Most of us are aware that a singular tweet is not the beginning of a beautiful friendship, but it can be a slippery slope.

Our brains are wired such that recognizing a face makes us feel as if we know a person, so when we see a star enough, we feel connected to her. And if we see a celebrity out of context—in a coffee shop instead of on TV, for instance—it can take a minute to figure out why he's so familiar. Once I was walking down Fifth Avenue when I saw a man approaching. I knew I knew him, but couldn't figure out how. He was an older, handsome guy. Was he a friend of my dad's? A teacher from my high school? We made eye contact, and I gave a friendly hello. I didn't want to be rude.

As we passed, I placed him. It was Paul McCartney.

Everyone I know has a parasocial relationship with somebody. Maybe she doesn't aspire to be just like that celebrity, but she thinks they could be best friends, or they'd have an instant love connection, or she's angry at said starlet for how a public breakup unraveled. Even Matt, my cool and collected husband, has one: with New England Patriots quarterback Tom Brady. He'll defend Brady against haters as if he's his brother. And he's got the admiration thing going, too. I swear he works out a little bit harder when watching his favorite player—or as Matt calls him, "the world's most handsome man"—on the field.

Parasocial relationships take much less work than the real kind. It's plenty easier to click on the TV and watch Ross, Rachel, and the gang in reruns than it is to coordinate schedules, plan a dinner, and go out for the evening with a friend. But face-to-face contact is vitally important. Parasocial relationships are not inter-changeable with the real-life kind, lest one become a recluse or, worse, that guy walking down the street talking to an imaginary friend.

Still, social scientists say parasocial relationships aren't com-pletely unhealthy. Research has shown that, when kept in check, we can reap the same benefits from an imagined relationship, like mine with Jennifer, as we do from the real-life kind. We might feel more connected, less isolated, and more confident. If we identify with someone, and also think highly of her, we might even by as-sociation think more highly of ourselves.

And there's something fun about these relationships, too. The act of referring to celebrities by their first names makes us feel glamorous, if only for a moment. It's an escape. When you're standing in the checkout line, waiting to pay for the same old gal-lon of milk and roll of toilet paper, catching up on the celebrity circuit as if you're an insider is a welcome diversion.

So it's fine to imagine that you'd fit right in on that girls' get-away vacation with Jennifer, Chelsea Handler, and Courteney Cox. Just as long as you don't buy a ticket.

* * *

On Day 21, things go off track. I sleep in. I take another preg-nancy test—still negative—which sends me directly to a bag of Reese's Pieces. I go to town on laziness. I watch three straight hours of TV. They say it takes three weeks to form a habit, which means I don't have this Aniston lifestyle nailed quite yet.

But things are moving in the right direction. A few days later, when I arrive at the gym for my babysitting shift, the owner gives me the once over. "You look good," she says. "There's something about you."

My celebrity glow, perhaps?

I keep that thought to myself. I'm not delusional, and I'm even a bit hesitant to admit I'm living a Life According to Jen. I haven't mastered the elevator pitch—how do you tell someone you are imitating (not stalking!) a Hollywood starlet?

But it's amazing to see the difference a few changes can make. Having developed the beginnings of a routine, I feel calmer. There is something resembling a muscle emerging in my arm. I'm more hydrated. Even more rested. Early to bed and early to rise provides a much better sleep than the 2 A.M. to 9:45 shift I'd been working.

And people are saying things. The other day Matt glanced at me in my skinny jeans and black top. "You're looking good," he said.

At book club, my friend Karen tilted her head and gave me that classic quizzical look. "You look great," she said. "Different."

"Thanks," I said. "I think this might be what happiness looks like."

One month in and I'm clearly feeling pleased with my progress. My clothes are fitting better and I've lost a few pounds. Running, weight lifting, and occasionally substituting fish and leafy greens for microwave meals and prepackaged snacks really does work. In fact, this whole pursuit would probably have an even more drastic effect, appearance-wise, if I could change my eating habits in proportion to how much I've altered my exercise. Intellectually, I know what I should be putting in my mouth, but practically, it's not computing. Dinners with friends are one culprit. There are also family gatherings, boredom snacking, and the daily 4 P.M. craving to contend with. For the past couple of months, on the day I've learned for sure, again, that I'm not pregnant, I've drowned my disappointment in a vat of chicken pad thai. This month was no different. And at the end of a particularly sugar-fueled weekend visiting Matt's mother in Cape Cod, Matt asked if I'd given up on my Jennifer-eating entirely.

"The struggle is part of the journey!" I explained.

"Then I hope you mention those four cookies you just ate in the book."

If I was a true celebrity, as opposed to an imposter, I could afford a personal chef. There's no need to eat out with friends when you can invite them over for a specially created meal, no prep work or cleanup required. But until I make my millions as a judge on *So You Think You Can Dance* (call me, Nigel Lythgoe!), my caloric consumption will be my cross to bear alone.

Obviously, there is still room for improvement on my journey. Aside from the food, the battle between Rachel and her alarm clock is ongoing. I still spend too much time in my pajama-exercise-clothes hybrid. But I'll get to those eventually. If the Jennifer Aniston portion of this quest is about fitness and a better body, and all the glorious trappings that go with that, perhaps I'm on my way. I'm certainly more confident. On the days I succeed in waking up early, doing some morning yoga, and showering before nine, I can faintly hear Katrina and the Waves singing "Walking on Sunshine" on the soundtrack of my life as I head out for my morning caffeine fix.

Working on improving myself might feel as good as actually *being* that improved version.

———

Another unexpected learning: There's something weirdly comforting in adopting a muse. In general, less thinking is required because the Jen-inspired guidelines eliminate some choice. Does this kind of behavior—no more free will! What Jen says goes!—border on cult worship? Sounds like it, but no. As long as I remember that Jennifer Aniston and I don't actually know each other—that she's not going to dump Courteney Cox or Chelsea Handler to be my BFF—I'm engaging in a sane, healthy level of admiration. According to the researchers who identified the condition known as Celebrity Worship Syndrome, things get weird only when you believe your parasocial relationship has become a personal connection with a star or, worse, when you go crazy-stalker on them.

Evolutionary biologists say that identifying and trying to emulate A-listers is totally normal. "Humans, unlike other species, obtain most of their information about the world from other humans," anthropologist Francisco Gil-White told ABC news. "We were selected . . . to rank successful individuals highly and to prefer them as models."

Does my life feel more generally fabulous and put-together? Yes. Somewhat. But no one is confusing me with Jennifer anytime soon. (And yes, I notice the full body scan I get when I tell people what I'm trying to do. As if there is nothing more impossible to believe than that I might achieve a celeb-like pair of legs.) And in some ways conquering one area just calls more attention to those where I fall short: the messy house, the unanswered emails, the pajamas-as-clothing.

And, again, the food. It's not only that I want to eat healthier—I want to cook more. I always feel better when eating a home-cooked meal, not only because it's less expensive and usually healthier but there's the accomplished feeling of having created something. And if there's anything that's become supertrendy among the celebrity folk these days, it's cooking. Superstars-turned-chefs include: Trisha Yearwood, Eva Longoria, Sheryl Crow, Patti LaBelle, Emilio Estefan (not Emilio Estevez, my original thought when I saw that byline and almost purchased what presumably would be the first ever *Breakfast Club Breakfast Cookbook*), Coolio, Jeff Foxworthy, Tony Danza, and Alicia Silverstone.

To take my food up a notch, I'll be following the gospel of arguably the foodiest—and most divisive—celebrity of all. The one who is building the next Stewart-esque empire by giving fans a glimpse into her kitchen, and who boasts Mario Batali and Jamie Oliver among her besties.

She's gorgeous. She's goopy. She's Gwyneth.

CHAPTER TWO

GWYNETH PALTROW'S KITCHEN

"If you're going to cook dinner, so that you and your husband can invest in each other, don't make duck à l'orange. Learn six recipes that are simple, easy, that you can do when you put the kids to bed."
—Vogue

"I love to cook and feed people. I cook every day."
—InStyle

"It's a perfectionist thing: 'This is going to be the best duck I've cooked,' or, 'This is going to be the best hour I've spent with my son.' I'm very hard on myself. It's exhausting."
—British GQ

The other day I was in a bookstore, explaining my current project to the manager. "I'm trying to celebrify myself," I explained, testing out a new verb. "I'm wondering, if I do what they do, will I feel as fabulous and put together as they seem to be?" This conversation usually goes one of two ways: Men stare blankly, women nod knowingly. Luckily, this manager was a woman. "I've been working on looking like Jennifer Aniston, can't you tell?" She smiled and laughed, knowing there was no right answer. "Next I'll be tackling Gwyneth Paltrow's kitchen."

"Oh, but Gwyneth isn't a real celebrity," she said.

Excuse me?

"She's so down-to-earth! With the cooking. And the kids."

"Well, she's definitely a celebrity," I said. "But if she makes you feel that way, then she's doing a great job with her branding."

While Jennifer Aniston seems to reject the idea that anyone should emulate her ("If somebody ever wished to be me for a day," she's been quoted as saying, "they'd be the most pissed-off person once they got here. They'd be, like, in hell.") Gwyneth Paltrow is the exact opposite. She has built an entire brand on the concept that people *should* want to be like her. Or, at least, they do, so why shouldn't she try to control the information out there. Better we live Gwyneth's life according to Gwyneth than Gwyneth's life according to TMZ.

Goop, Gwyneth's popular website and email newsletter, was created, it says, to "share all of life's positives. From creating a delicious recipe to finding a perfect dress for spring, Gwyneth began curating the best of lifestyle to help her readers save time, simplify and feel inspired." Knowing that legions of women would kill to be her best friend, Gwyneth created the next best thing. At least according to her. ". . . For many, Goop has become their most trusted girlfriend on the web," she boasts on the site.

I'm not sure I'd go that far, but Goop certainly is a fountain of live-like-Gwyneth gold. With a few clicks of my mouse I can dress like her (I especially love her "what to wear on a flight" issue), work out like her (exclusive videos from Tracy Anderson, her personal trainer) and, most important for me, cook like her.

Any movie star gallivanting around the Internet as if she's a commoner is bound to draw criticism, and the site has as many haters as worshippers. Posts about how one *must* stay at La Mamounia in Marrakesh or spend $90 for "The Goop tee" perpetuate the idea that Gwyneth is completely out of touch with the trials of normal women. Buzzfeed.com did an entire post on the

"7 Reasons Why People Hate Gwyneth Paltrow," which included quotes like "I'd rather die than let my kids eat Cup-a-Soup" and "I am obsessed with chopped salad." *Star* magazine named her Hollywood's Most Hated Celebrity. She is a constant reminder of everything we think we should be doing but are not. A reporter I met recently told me Goop should be outlawed. "As if I have time to spend days preparing duck for my kids," she said.

Even I, who has concocted an entire lifestyle out of trying to emulate the stars, have moments of turnoff. In a *Vogue* interview with food writer Jeffrey Steingarten, Gwyneth spoke endlessly of her two pizza ovens—as in *two* outdoor ovens, completely separate from her regular indoor kitchen ovens, solely for the purpose of making pizza. This is neither normal nor attainable, and doesn't seem deserving of so much real estate in an interview that will largely be read by the plebeian non-pizza-oven-owning public.

In the same story, this happens: Steingarten writes, "Would she rather have somebody else's body? Did she hate any part of her own, the way Nora Ephron had written about how much she hated her own neck?" Gwyneth can't answer. "I'll have to give that a little thought," she tells him. Which at first makes me sort of hate her—who can't think of something she doesn't like about her own body? I can hardly think of something I *do* like on my body!

But then I remember that she is Gwyneth Paltrow, with Gwyneth Paltrow's looks. And if Gwyneth Paltrow can't be pleased with every last inch of herself, then there's no hope for any of us. So maybe I love her for being confident and not perpetuating the body-hatred thing. Either, or.

During my hours of Gwyneth research I write Matt an email, telling him to save the date three Sundays from now for "a Gwyneth-style duck feast." That reporter might not have time to spend days preparing a perfect Chinese roasted duck, but I'll make time if I have to.

Aside from Goop, I've been poring over Ms. Paltrow's first cookbook, *My Father's Daughter*, and I actually feel rather inspired. Six years ago, when Matt and I first moved to Chicago, I cooked a lot. I was between jobs, had no friends in my new city, and decided to teach myself to cook. I achieved this by putting together almost every Rachael Ray 30-minute meal out there. Matt was a happy camper.

And then I made new friends. Cooking nights were abandoned in exchange for dinners and outings with potential pals. While Matt was certainly pleased to have a happy wife, one who didn't constantly complain about being lonely, I know he missed those homemade meals. He never said so outright, but enough side comments about how "Rachel used to cook" made the point for him. (I should note that home-cooked meals were never so important to Matt that he was moved to cook for himself. Matt can make pasta, and sausage, and pasta with sausage.)

For the past couple of years, cooking has largely been replaced with microwave or restaurant-prepped meals. But now that my new friends are becoming old friends, I'd love to trade those nights of eating out for at-home dinner parties. Many of Gwyneth's recipes seem more suited to group meals than a simple Wednesday night dinner for two, and just the act of reading her pages makes me feel like those gatherings are within my reach. The other day I sat on the couch and watched an entire workout DVD on the computer. I didn't actually do any exercise, but just watching those guys sweat made me feel accomplished by osmosis. This is similar. Reading a cookbook makes me feel like a cook.

A cook who can conquer a duck feast.

Matt writes back a two-word email, but that's all it takes for me to know he's excited about the new celebrity in our lives: "Duck feast!!!"

My first stop in the world of glamorous Paltrow-style eating and cooking must be, of course, the farmer's market. Happy, together, oh-this-old-thing-I-whipped-it-up-in-my-pizza-oven celebrities wouldn't be caught dead shopping in the mainstream processed-food-ridden supermarkets that I frequent. They'll go to Whole Foods—if *Us Weekly* is to be believed they convene there for a weekly town hall meeting—but only if they have to. First choice—just ask Gwynnie—is the farmer's market.

My friend Genny and I head to Chicago's Green City Market on a Saturday morning. I'm wearing a blue striped romper, with my canvas tote bag in one hand and *My Father's Daughter* in the other. I've never actually worn this romper in public, at least not in a town where I might see someone I know. I bought it for my Croatian honeymoon and haven't put it on since. But its souped-up-overalls vibe feels very farmer, and certainly like something Gwyneth would throw on for a trip to grab fresh tomatoes in London or L.A. Lately, picking out the perfect outfit to emulate a star's "I threw this on as I ran out the door" look is taking up way too much of my time. It takes far more effort to pull together an "effortlessly cool" outfit than it does to style a look for even a black-tie wedding. Fancy affairs have such clear rules. Cool *and* casual still confuses me.

For today, the romper definitely screams Gwyneth. And so I've decided to take a fashion risk. I can't decide whether to be nervous or excited to run into a familiar face. Probably a little of both.

"You look so market-ready," Genny says when she picks me

up. Her ten-month-old daughter, Camille, is in the car too, and there's no better farmer's market accessory than a baby. Strollers are the vehicle of choice at the Green City Market, so we'll fit right in.

"Well, not as ready as Camille," I tell Genny. "Look at her! She's so big." I haven't seen Genny's daughter in a few months— too long—and she looks like a different person.

"When are you going to make a little one of your own?" Genny asks.

"Soon, I hope," I say. "We've been trying, but it hasn't been going well." I used to be secretive about this baby question, but I've decided to open up more, at least with close friends. I constantly remind myself that there's no shame in having trouble, even though it feels like a dirty secret. Making a baby is the goal I'm failing most miserably at, and though I know it's not my fault—or anyone's fault—the failure feels personal. Maybe talking about the struggle will help my frustration, and remind me that taking up to a year to get pregnant is relatively normal.

When mere acquaintances ask about our baby plans, I'm more evasive. I hate lying, but I also don't want to let everyone in on my very personal quest. Is it necessary to tell my husband's co-worker, for example, that so far it hasn't taken, but he's stopped taking hot baths and we're hoping that will help his swimmers? I don't think so.

For the first four months after Matt and I decided we were ready, I was pretty levelheaded. I knew it could take a while and that plenty of people didn't get pregnant on the first or second try. But over the next four months, the feelings of sadness and defeat crept in. I want a baby more than I've ever wanted anything—certainly more than Jennifer's body or Gwyneth's kitchen. And yet, these days, those celebrity dreams seem far more attainable. One thing I hadn't known when we started this pregnancy journey is that once you realize you want a baby, you want that baby yesterday. At least, that's been my experience. Now that I've let myself think about our child in the tangible sense—not just the one-day-when-we-grow-up-and-have-kids theoretical sense—I feel an incredible sense of longing. I want to meet him. Or her. It's as if I've flipped the switch on my deepest maternal instincts, and suddenly there's a tidal wave of untapped emotion building, ready to engulf someone who hasn't even been conceived yet.

It's surprisingly overwhelming.

I tell Genny that Matt and I have been trying for eight months now and that I didn't expect to be riding such an emotional roller coaster. I reiterate the complaints that all women who have trouble getting pregnant share: That I spent so long making sure I wouldn't get pregnant that it never occurred to me this would be the hard part. That I can't figure out why I spent so much money on birth control for the last decade. That everywhere I turn it seems others are getting knocked up on the first try, or by accident, and I feel taunted by the strollers that roll past my window in droves. That my middle school health teacher definitely hammered home that sex-baby conditional: *if* unprotected sex, *then* pregnancy, and I never realized how tough it could actually be. I'm not saying this is the wrong way to teach kids—I'm certainly glad I was careful until now—but learning that the window per cycle to actually get pregnant is something like 48 hours a month was a bit of a shocker.

"It's amazing how much you don't know until you're in it, isn't it?" Genny asks, looking back at Camille. "But that doesn't change."

My intention at the farmer's market is to fill up on Gwyneth's must-haves. There are a lot of them. The list of "Essential Food Items to Keep In Your Kitchen" is 86 items long and includes some obvious pantry staples—olive oil, salt, baking soda—and even more eccentric ones. I doubt everyone would put Vegenaise (vegan mayo), bomba rice for paella, bonita flakes, or pumpkin seeds on their list of kitchen necessities, but Gwyneth isn't just anyone. Another list of essentials enumerates the nineteen tools a home-cook should have, and while that wood-burning oven isn't listed, other financial investments, like a Le Creuset Dutch Oven and Vitamix blender, are. Luckily, I received the Le Creuset pot as well as a KitchenAid mixer (another apparent must) when I got married, but the Vitamix blender (about $400) and KitchenAid pasta roller attachment ($200) will have to wait. I have a blender already, and unless I grow so attached to cooking like Gwyneth that *My Father's Daughter* becomes one of those dog-eared, tattered tomes that I hand down to my daughter and my daughter's daughter, I just don't believe I'll cook enough homemade pasta to make a pasta roller worth it. My cabinet filled with barely used kitchen gadgets (did I really need a griddle/panini press in addition to my grill pan? And will someone please teach me how to use my mandoline?) pretty much confirms that.

More than I ever did during my month focused on Jennifer Aniston, I'm already feeling the monetary strain of not being a celebrity during this season of Gwyneth. As much as I'd love a backyard pizza stove, my wallet (and nonexistent backyard) won't allow it. I just don't have the funds to do everything that is called for to cook, eat, and entertain like my muse. It's frustrating, because I'm a pretty all-or-nothing kind of person. If I'm going to embark on a quest that calls for cooking like Gwyneth, I want to do that. Exactly.

I get the sense that Gwyneth herself is pretty similar on the all-or-nothing scale. She freely admits to being a perfectionist, and I bet if she were undertaking this project, she wouldn't let a measly issue like cost stand in her way. Part of me is definitely wondering if it's worth living like Gwyneth if I can't actually live like Gwyneth. But that's the point of this whole quest. I want to know how close I can come to a celebrity life given my Joe Schmo constraints. And to see if that watered-down version of celebrity living will still make me feel fabulous, composed, and altogether happier. So, I decide to get what I can from the list and go from there. "Do what you can" might be the overarching theme to a life glamorously lived.

A couple of hours later, I'm in my kitchen with my purchases: Carrots, blueberry preserves, blueberries, cherries, onions, tomatoes, fresh basil, and mozzarella from the farmer's market; frozen peas, olive oil, celery, and a leek from my local grocery store. I've already cleaned out my refrigerator and pantry, dumping expired or processed food, and many, many old beer cans. Now that my fridge has been Gwynethized, it looks like something out of *Real Simple*. Basically bare, save for a crisper drawer full of veggies, and plates full of washed cherries and blueberries. There's some cheese, a few beer bottles, and that's about it. Just looking at it gives me a rush of self-righteous satisfaction.

I spend the afternoon making vegetable stock, a "freezer essential," and slow-roasted tomatoes. It's all so civilized.

Tonight I have plans with my friend Liz. Instead of suggesting the usual dinner of delivery sushi or pizza, I tell her I'm going to make Gwyneth's Pea and Basil soup. She's thrilled, as the meal is both inexpensive and diet-friendly. I'm hoping this will become a theme in my relationships as I become Goopier. I want to cook and entertain like Gwyneth, and hopefully others are just as happy to sit back and be fed.

As Liz makes her way down the hallway to my apartment, the look on her face is a mix of surprise and confusion.

"Is that smell coming from *your* apartment?" she asks.

"It just might be," I say. "I'm making you soup, using home-made vegetable broth. You should feel very important." I need to revel in my first bits of Gwyneth success, even if making soup is hardly a newsworthy feat.

The soup is delicious, and the weeks to come are filled with more dinners, cooked to varying degrees of success. Ten-hour chicken, homemade veggie burgers (more like homemade veggie sloppy joes, but that's what happens when you misunderstand "½ cup cooked brown rice" and end up with three times more grains than necessary in your rice-and-bean mixture), Indian-spiced tuna steaks, fish tacos, broiled salmon with homemade teriyaki sauce, and more.

On the night of our first official Gwyneth meal together, after Matt and I feasted on a dinner of ten-hour chicken (a tender and juicy slow-cooked bird with crispy skin) and carmelized brussels sprouts, he nodded his approval. "I think I'm going to like this phase much better than Jennifer Aniston."

Not that I've given up on Jennifer. I'm still doing my two-a-day workouts, going to the gym first thing and then doing an at-home exercise—yoga, pilates or, now, Tracy Anderson Method—in the evening. Tracy Anderson is the brain behind the Paltrow body. The woman who, according to Gwyneth, "kicked my formerly sagging ass into shape." (I can't remember her ass ever sagging, but I guess it's all relative.) Anderson has provided a few free workout videos for Goop and has some on YouTube as well, so I've incorporated them into my living room exercise rotation. The good news: They're short. The less good news: They hurt.

For those keeping track, that's about one-and-a-half to two hours of working out each day, plus at least an hour spent cooking most days. If cost is already the biggest restriction on my celebrity-esque life, time is a close second. I really do like *My Father's Daughter*, not just because it's Gwyneth's cookbook but because the food I've made has tasted good, looked impressive, and made me feel like something of a chef. But so few of the recipes are quick, weekday meals. The subtitle of the cookbook is "Delicious, Easy Recipes Celebrating Family & Togetherness," but most of the dishes I want to make appear too complicated or time-consuming for your average weeknight. Recipes like whole roasted fish or duck cassoulet or seafood paella feel daunting rather than inviting, and make me question what Gwyneth knows about the plight of the everygirl who wants to cook dinner after a long day's work. I'm lucky to do my job from home, which affords me the freedom to marinate a salmon in the fridge for a few hours before we eat, or get the ten-hour chicken prepped at 10 A.M. so dinner is ready at a reasonable hour, but even I can tell that fitting in all my fabulous life requirements will be a sticking point as this quest progresses.

I'm not saying Gwyneth has more time than the rest of us, or that she doesn't know what a hard day's work is. I very much believe she does (you don't get that many hyphenates in your job description without logging long hours) but cooking is part of her job. And being fit is arguably Jennifer Aniston's number one career requirement. I want to look and feel fabulous like both of them, to give my life the glimmer of perfection that makes me feel I've got it all figured out, but the time it takes to get there is even more than I anticipated. I knew I'd spend time working out and cooking, but my vision was some romanticized version of the photos I see in *People* magazine's Star Tracks. I never really thought about the hours logged at the grocery store, or the twenty-five-minute trafficky drive back from Whole Foods because where else can a person find vegan mayonnaise? We all know that time is one of the biggest deterrents to so many of the habits we'd like to adopt—working out, cooking, decluttering, meditating, sleeping well—but deep down I always thought I simply wasn't working hard enough to fit it all in. If I focused and took action rather than merely gawking at the celebrities I revered, my fabulous life would fall into place. How hard could it be, really? Now that I'm doing it, let me tell you: Action takes time. And no matter what you're doing, add a half hour. My workout class is an hour, but getting there five minutes early, dawdling afterward, and walking back and forth from home adds about thirty minutes. I've never, not once, cooked a recipe in the duration allotted in the instructions. It's a time-sucking business, this living well.

* * *

Gwyneth is only one of many stars who has used her fabulous lifestyle to build a brand, and I'm not sure whether this is a great thing (if we're going to emulate celebrities anyway, at least now they're making it easier) or obnoxious self-indulgence. *Fame Junkies* author Jake Halpern says it's merely a reflection of the power shift in Hollywood. "Back in the studio days, movie stars were totally at the mercy of studio bosses," he tells me over the phone one day. "Now the big celebrities are their own mini-corporations. It doesn't really make sense to think of yourself as just an actress, or just a sports star, anymore. Of course there are people who do that—Jeremy Irons or Judi Dench, maybe—but agents and managers are telling stars that they want to branch out as much as possible, not just be confined to the realm of their immediate talent." So of course Mariah Carey should have a perfume, and Justin Bieber should have a nail polish. Why not?

It should come as no big surprise that this boom in celebrity obsession—and the lifestyles that come with—is happening now, Halpern says. If it started with the onslaught of tween magazines like *Bop,* the timing is right on target. *Bop,* you may remember, is the *Tiger Beat*–esque magazine that launched in 1983. It was light on content and heavy on fold-out posters, but the few articles it did have made you feel like Jonathan Taylor Thomas or Joey Lawrence might possibly be your next boyfriend. *Bop* was my very first magazine subscription, and I plastered my walls with its posters of Kirk Cameron and Mark-Paul Gosselaar, and even Alyssa Milano, my girl crush before that was even a phrase. *Bop* was a magazine for ten-year-olds and up, so its very first fans are now in their thirties and forties. "The generation that grew up with those magazines have carried the celebrity-centric mind-set into adulthood," Halpern points out.

That mind-set, he says, includes living vicariously through celebrities. When we were preteens we wanted to be just like the members of the Mickey Mouse Club, but that's not so different from our current fantasies of living as fabulously as their adult counterparts. Older generations might have been fascinated with the *National Enquirer*'s take on the rich and famous, but the new world of celebrity obsession is more about feeling close to stars than rooting for their downfall. "When you're at the checkout line in the grocery store, you have two choices for how you want to look at celebrities: the *Us Weekly* version and the *National En-*

quirer version," Halpern says. "They are two vastly different renderings of the same thing, and it's a question of what you want to buy into. What do you want out of this? Do you want to have a feel-good experience where you see celebrities depicted in this intimate positive way, being told they're just like you and you're on a first-name basis, the way you would hear an update on your friends and what's going on in their lives? Or do you want to hear that they have bulimia, they just got divorced, they lost their kids, they have drug addictions, and think to yourself, 'That's so messed up. As bad as my life may be it is not nearly as bad as that,' and take some prurient pleasure in the misfortune of other people? We use these magazines for whatever we want." And these days we want to feel better about ourselves by feeling connected with celebrities, Halpern argues, rather than feeling superior to them. That these magazines sometimes have the opposite effect, making us feel worse about ourselves as we compare our lot to the stars', Halpern says, is an unfortunate by-product.

The celebrity as lifestyle guru isn't so much a good or bad thing as an inevitable one. It's a natural next move for celebrities looking to capitalize on their fame and influence. If their fans want to feel connected, why shouldn't stars give the people what they want? And not all celebrities look at their fame as simply a moneymaker. Many use their notoriety to give back to the community or raise awareness for worthy causes. Look at Angelina Jolie, whose 2013 decision to have a preventative double mastectomy—and to speak publicly about it—shined a giant spotlight on women's health issues.

"To some extent we all need people who inspire us, whether it's Winston Churchill or Gwyneth Paltrow," Halpern tells me. "If you are inspired to make yourself a better person, there's nothing wrong with where it comes from. There were probably kids inspired by Alexander the Great or Cleopatra—it's inherently human. The question is, are the things that you are striving for really things that are going to make you happier and more productive? And are you maintaining a healthy form of separation? I may admire Hemingway, and there may be some value in aspiring to be like him, but if I'm going to beat myself up when I don't live up to those incredible standards, that's another thing. It can quickly become unhealthy."

That conundrum—how to be inspired by my muses without being disappointed in myself when I don't reach their levels of fabulousness—will likely be the crux of this whole pursuit.

* * *

The "togetherness" part of the *My Father's Daugher* subtitle rings true for me. The recipes in this book have me excited to cook for company, so I've turned the duck feast—originally planned for just Matt and me—into my first official dinner party. The menu à la Gwyneth: Best Miso Soup, Perfect Chinese Roasted Duck (complete with homemade sesame pancakes and homemade red miso hoisin sauce), and Fried Rice with Kale.

I set my alarm for 7:45 on Saturday morning to begin cooking for the Sunday-night meal. This is unusually early for my weekend routine, but the duck prep will take about three hours, and that's before I marinate it overnight. We're going to a wedding reception this afternoon and have dinner plans tonight, so if I want to serve this meal tomorrow, I need to start cooking.

Over the course of the next two days, I cook whenever I'm home. After the wedding, I spend an hour making sesame pancakes and invite Matt to try one.

"It's good," he says, "but is it done?"

"I don't understand the question."

"It's kind of boring," he says. "This is your only side dish?"

"It's not a side dish. You put the slices of duck on it, like a taco, with the hoisin sauce," I explain, feeling like quite the chef. "I'm making a rice-and-kale dish as the side."

"Oh, then it's delicious."

When our company arrives on Sunday evening, I've set the table (using actual cloth napkins!), cleaned the house, put the duck in the oven, and have the soup warming on the stove. I wonder if this is what the Paltrow-Martin household looks like on a random Tuesday evening.

The dinner is a rousing success consisting of many glasses of wine and even more Chinese duck tacos. At about 9 P.M., my seventy-five-year-old neighbor knocks on the door to borrow our phone—his is out of service and he has to call the friend who checks in on him every night, to let her know he's alive—and stays to eat cupcakes and regale us with stories of his family tree. It's a memorable evening, and has me convinced that my thirty-year-old self is more suited to at-home company with a few bottles of wine than going out to bars with all of twenty-something Chicago.

Dinner parties are the new pub crawls.

At the end of the evening, while walking our guests out, I pass Gwyneth's cookbook open on the kitchen counter.

"All this work, and I still look nothing like her," I say.

"That's because you don't look anything like Gwyneth Paltrow," Matt says.

I give my husband the death stare. "That is the meanest thing you've ever said to me."

* * *

If my (parasocial) relationship with Jennifer was one of strict admiration and aspiration, my feelings for Gwyneth have become more mixed. Yes, I love what she's done for my kitchen. But the more I research—reading profiles and Goop newsletters, watching interviews—the more I commiserate with both the Gwyneth lovers and the haters. It's as if Jennifer is the one I want to be friends with, while Gwyneth is that untouchable popular girl who I simultaneously adore and abhor. She seems more intimidating than Jen, certainly. In this imaginary celebrity high school scenario, I'd be scared to talk to Gwynnie, lest I should wear or eat something wrong in her presence and she got all "why-are-you-talking-to-me-peasant?" on me.

But then, perhaps I'm overthinking it.

I say all this because every time I open a Goop newsletter, or watch an interview clip, I'm overcome with that initial sense of "what world does she think we live in?" I can't justify buying the pricey clothes Gwyneth sells on Goop, and, while I don't have kids yet, I can guarantee I will let my children watch English-language TV, whereas Gwyneth says she only lets Apple and Moses watch in French or Spanish.

Still, obviously, there is something in Gwyneth I keep coming back to. I love creating my culinary existence in her image. I'll never pen a cookbook of my own, and yet I've made great strides in the kitchen. It's amazing how far a home-cooked meal can go toward making a girl feel like her hectic life is more in balance. Eating microwave meals out of cardboard containers, even if the dishes are made with organic ingredients, will never feel glamorous.

I also relish reading about the fabulous shops Gwyneth frequents in London, her weekly blowouts from her hairstylist (a time-saver for any working mom, she says), and her dinner parties with Beyoncé and Jay Z. No, they aren't relatable, but neither was *Lifestyles of the Rich and Famous* and that was on TV for nine seasons (though Robin Leech didn't purport to be giving advice for saving time and simplifying). The point is, women aren't reading Goop for real-life, immediately implementable tips on how to conquer life on a budget. We read for an inside peek at how the other half lives. We want to know what Gwyneth's life is like when she's not on-screen, and we want to see if there is anything we can do to feel a bit more like a celebrity ourselves.

Ultimately, it's Gwyneth's whole perfect-specimen image, one that she claims any woman can achieve with just a little effort, that has the entire celebrity-consuming world fascinated by her. She's the first to say that she only looks as good as she does because she works for it. Gwyneth once told *USA Today* that "the reason that I can be 38 and have two kids and wear a bikini is because I work my fucking ass off. It's not an accident. It's not luck, it's not fairy dust, it's not good genes. It's killing myself for an hour and a half five days a week, but what I get out of it is relative to what I put into it. That's what I try to do in all areas of my life." And that's where the love-hate reaction comes in. I feel inspired that if maybe I work harder I too can feel fabulous in "all areas of my life." But I'm also insulted at the notion that the reason I don't feel perfect is that I don't *do* enough, rather than because I don't have her money or her staff or her access.

Rihanna, who is the object of many fans' worship herself, probably summed it up best when she told a pair of radio hosts that "I'm really jealous of [Gwyneth], I don't even know why I like her."

* * *

I've been cooking like Gwyneth for a few weeks now, not to mention working out like her and putting her wear-a-blazer-whenever-you-travel tips to use, and I'm no closer to morphing into a leggy blonde with unnaturally glowing skin. Nor do I look like any sort of Jennifer-Gwyneth hybrid that would make a conference room full of *Maxim* editors' brains explode. But more important than looks, I don't *feel* anything like the way I imagine Gwyneth does on a daily basis.

From the various interviews I've seen and the Goop newsletters I've read, my impression is that Gwyneth goes through life floating on air. Literally. I picture her getting from the gym to the movie studio via cloud, upon which she sits meditatively in lotus position. There's this contentedness about her that's really compelling, as if she's supremely confident in exactly what she has, doesn't want for anything more, and is simply at peace.

There's only one logical way for me to attain this Zen state for myself.

I'm doing Gwyneth's cleanse.

The seven-day detox outlined in a 2008 edition of Goop was designed as an "elimination diet" to help Gwyneth and her flock lose a few pounds of holiday excess and gain energy. It's summer around here, but the principles are the same. Despite my increased activity in the kitchen—and the relative healthfulness of most of Gwyneth's recipes—my body could certainly use a restart. I've been trying to keep up my Jen eating habits, and the two celebs are fairly aligned in their endorsement of natural green foods and lots of salmon, but the whole eating—or lack thereof—is still the hardest part of this quest for me. First of all, every recipe venture is accompanied by a glass of wine. (It's a direct order, per the cookbook: "Invest in what's real. Clean as you go. Drink while you cook.") I think my weekly alcohol intake has significantly increased since I started with Gwen and Jen. Secondly, I've been eating duck for three days now—Gwyneth instructed that I *must* make the duck soba soup the day after the roast, and then there was a day of leftovers—and it was a cap to a week of rich, indulgent eats. They were natural and straight from the farmer's market, but the farmer's market sells cookies, too. It's not all from-the-ground stuff.

I've cleansed once before, two years ago. It was a less extreme cleanse than Goop's, but longer. The best I can say: I didn't hate it. That I'm willingly signing on for another speaks for itself.

The menu for this detox is mostly liquid—smoothie for breakfast and soup for dinner, with some chewing at lunchtime. The grocery list for day one alone is long, and probably pricey, so I'm shopping for only a day at a time. That way, if I don't make it past the inaugural meal plan, I won't have wasted my hard-earned cash on too many boxes of coconut water. I don't want to kick off the cleanse with a defeatist attitude, or set myself up to fail; it's just that I might get defeated and fail.

If I can make it through this weeklong diet, I have high hopes that it will help me feel physically and emotionally lighter, clear my skin, shine my hair, and induce me into a calm, quiet state. The one thing I enjoyed about my first detox attempt was that my energy flatlined, but in a good way. There were none of the spikes and dives that usually result from my caffeine addiction. Still, I'll admit I'm terrified. There are a number of reasons for this. First, the sheer look of the menu. It's sparse. I like food. I really like chewing. Neither of which are offered in abundance here. Instead, most breakfasts consist of two different types of powder, not the usual form in which I take my nutrients. There's also the fact that I'll have to give up Diet Coke for a week, which I'm assuming will cause some serious headaches. And third, I don't want to stop working out. (Look, Jen! It's a new me!) My gym classes are fairly rigorous, and the type that probably call for nutritional fuel.

I owe my biggest concerns, though, to Gwyneth's detox specialist. In that cleanse-themed issue of Goop, Dr. Alejandro Junger warns: "If your bowel movements get sluggish, you can accelerate things by drinking half a shot glass of castor oil followed by a glass of water or using a mild herbal laxative. Bowel elimination is paramount for correct detoxification." Without getting into too much detail, I can tell you I've never had any trouble in that area, and the thought of creating a struggle that only a swig of castor oil can fix sounds wretched.

Internet research tells me that bloggers and other writers who have tried the cleanse almost all bailed early, which also doesn't inspire confidence that I'll make it through the weeklong run. Here's what is working in my favor: I'm determined. I'm usually pretty gung ho about sticking to a project. I love conquering a challenge.

And anyway, if I want a taste of the good life, I guess I need to swallow the gross bits, too.

The grocery list for day one includes almond milk, coconut water, what seems like forty different types of greens, and the two protein powders. I end up spending $40 at my local grocery store and another $40 at the health food store where I buy whey protein powder and a green powder with probiotics. The powders should last me the whole week, but $40 a day on food is a hefty price tag. Here's hoping one bunch of arugula can satisfy two meal plans.

My friend Kari and I worked together during my last cleanse, and she has borne witness to a number of my food "kicks." The no-sugar week, the numerous caffeine bans I've unsuccessfully imposed, the two-week South Beach Phase One wedding diet that I followed for seven weeks. In fact, it was Kari's husband who spurred me to go gluten-free one week after he explained that cutting out gluten was what made Novak Djokovic shoot to number one in the world tennis rankings. ("If you didn't eat gluten, you would have written ten books by now!")

Tonight we're going to dinner, where I plan on ingesting some serious protein to prep for the week ahead. "I'm going on a Gwyneth cleanse," I tell Kari.

"What does that entail?"

"Lots of liquids. Tomorrow I'll have a smoothie for breakfast, a salad for lunch, and soup for dinner. And some pumpkin seeds for a snack," I say. "Also there are many powders."

Kari's eyebrows wrinkle in horror. "No offense," she says, "but I'm glad we don't work together anymore. I don't want to fall victim to hungry Rachel's wrath."

Cleanse day one starts with a workout—Dr. Junger says I must sweat to get rid of toxins—and then a smoothie. One and a half cups of almond milk, a half cup of blueberries, one scoop of the whey protein powder, one scoop of the green powder. Blend and serve.

When I take the lid off my blender and take a peek at what I've made, I immediately get the chills. First of all, the drink is green. Not that bright encouraging green like a smoothie you'd get at Jamba Juice or the drink that Dr. Oz is always touting. This one looks like seaweed. Again, not the seaweed you'd get in a lovely seaweed salad at your favorite neighborhood sushi restaurant. It reminds me of the slimy dark stuff that finds my feet at the bottom of the ocean. It smells like it too. (I read later that this powder does indeed contain algae and "sea vegetables including kelp," which apparently people like Gwyneth and Dr. Junger take to be a good thing.) But worse than all of that, the issue that has me backing away in fear, is that my smoothie is moving. *Moving.* I know the green powder is filled with "active probiotic cells," but I didn't realize they'd be so active that my breakfast would be alive.

It only takes one sip to know I won't be able to get this down. Not like this at least. It tastes like really sweet earwax.

The fact that we eat first with our other senses—sight, smell—isn't helping.

There are very few foods in this world that I can't eat, but this drink isn't going to happen, at least not at room temperature, and not with the thick layer of jumpy foam that has settled at the top of my glass.

I add three ice cubes and place the smoothie in the fridge.

Five minutes later, I launch attempt number two. The drink is cold. The foam has been scraped off. I try another sip, and my gag reflex kicks in. Does Gwyneth really drink this? I have trouble picturing her throwing back a glassful while wrangling Apple and Moses for school. I feel duped—why didn't she warn us Goopers that breakfast would taste like urine and smell like rotten fish?

In the battle of Rachel vs. the smoothie, the smoothie has won. I dump it out, make another with only almond milk and blueberry, and move on.

The rest of the day goes more smoothly, even if, again, these tasks demand too many hours. Between the breakfast smoothie and the carrot-ginger dressing I have to make for my lunch salad, I spend some ninety minutes in the kitchen chopping, blending, and cleaning up. All before noon. But lunch is good, and the broccoli and arugula soup (ingredients: arugula, broccoli, onion, garlic, water) is actually pretty tasty. The major headline, on the positive side, is that I don't particularly miss my Diet Coke. I drink a box of coconut water throughout the day and am pretty satisfied.

By the end of the day the smoothie disaster seems like a bad but distant memory. Still, I'm more tired than usual, so I climb into bed at 9:45.

"I can totally handle this cleanse," I tell Matt as I settle under the covers. "I hardly missed the caffeine, I have no headache, and I'm not even hungry."

Famous last words.

The next morning it all goes south. I wake up with a low-level headache. Despite having slept ten hours last night, I'm in a fog and have no energy, so I pass on my morning workout. Instead, I head back to the grocery store to get the ingredients for day two—rice milk for the breakfast smoothie; chicken, agave syrup, and balsamic vinegar for the lunchtime "detox teriyaki chicken." $35. Luckily for my wallet, the miso soup 4 P.M. snack uses all the same ingredients I bought for the duck dinner party, and I decide to eat last night's leftover broccoli soup for dinner rather than invest in the ingredients for day two's pea-and-basil version. The day's prep time is even longer—I have to make teriyaki sauce for the chicken, plus the miso soup broth. I don't know how someone who works full days in an office could ever have the time to get all this together.

I make my breakfast smoothie with blueberries, rice milk, and the whey protein powder, assuming it was the green stuff that made breakfast so unbearable yesterday. It's better—there's nothing crawling in my glass this time—but my resolve is lower. The sweetness of the powder makes me nauseous, so I try again, this time with only berries and rice milk, nearly the same as yesterday.

Maybe it's my headache, maybe it's hunger, maybe it's the memory of that first smoothie debacle, but today I can't get even this one down. After three sips I dump it into the sink.

A couple of hours later, my head feels worse, the nausea hasn't subsided, and I can hardly keep my eyes open to look at the computer. I call Matt.

"I think I might be dying," I say, practically in tears. "I can't get any work done because the computer screen gives me a headache. Plus, it's Friday. I'm supposed to go out with friends tonight and I don't know how I will get through a weekend living like this. I'm going to be horrible company. I may not even survive."

There is a slight chance I'm being melodramatic. Hunger does that to a person.

"Just stop doing it," Matt says. He's a cheerleader for my projects, and was in favor of my cleanse attempt, but no one wants to live with a wife near tears for a week. "You tried and it didn't work."

"But I have five more days," I insist.

"Do what you want, but it's stupid to suffer just to suffer. At least take some Advil."

The painkillers don't work. I lie on my couch, contemplating my options. I could power through, likely enduring an increasingly torturous headache for at least a few more days. I'll be terrible company to my friends, with whom I'd made plans long before I decided to detox. Who wants to go to dinner with someone who doesn't eat? Or have a girls' night with a friend who can't keep her eyes open? And I'll be useless to my sister-in-law, whom I promised to join for a three-hour mini-triathlon workout extravaganza tomorrow. I'd also have to pass on exercise for the rest of the week, since I wouldn't get enough calories to sustain high-intensity interval workouts, though Dr. Junger did recommend gentle yoga.

I must choose between being Jennifer and being Gwyneth. The nine-times-a-week workouts and 700-calorie days cannot co-exist peacefully.

The decision is easy. One organic black-bean-and-corn enchilada and two-hour nap later, I feel human again. A bit like a quitter of a human, but still human.

* * *

Maybe I should have expected this, but a side effect of my quest is that I'm getting even more obsessive about celebrity culture as the days go by. I used to check out the paparazzi photos on People.com once a week; now it's more like once a day. And I'm increasingly sizing myself up according to the stars, which is both dangerous and not all that happiness-inducing. After reading that Carrie Underwood writes down every morsel she puts in her mouth, or clicking through forty-four slides of celebrity bikini bodies on Foxnews.com, I feel less motivated and confident, rather than more.

It's a slippery slope, this celebrity-as-muse endeavor. Former *Us Weekly* editor Janice Min said it best in her *New York Times* article, "Can a Mom Get a Break?" She was writing specifically about America's obsession with "body after baby" but her sentiments hold true across the board: "Let's face it: celebrities aren't always terrible examples; many eat well, exercise and dress far cuter than we do. They've learned how to pull it together," she writes. "Still, our tendency toward these extremes makes us a self-loathing bunch." This, after Min published her first book, *How to*

Look Hot in a Mini-Van: A Real Woman's Guide to Losing Weight, Looking Great, and Dressing Chic in the Age of the Celebrity Mom. The title, not to mention the gallery of full-color photos of Heidi Klum or Gisele Bundchen looking stunning and slim just after giving birth, does its part to encourage the exact type of self-loathing she writes of.

The worldwide obsession with celebrity is ever increasing, and America's got it bad. Once upon a time, we adored the likes of Marilyn Monroe or Gene Kelly for their talent (and, yes, good looks) on-screen. But we didn't turn to them for dinner advice or to figure out how many crunches we should be doing. They weren't doubling as our interior decorators or parenting experts. Research shows that the modern cult of celebrity began in the eighteenth century. According to a study out of the University of Warwick, "the sudden rise in the popularity of obituaries of un-usual people in the 1700s provided people with the 18th century equivalent of a celebrity magazine." The researchers claim that the rise in popularity of obituaries was because the people featured in the death notices were "objects of scandal and public fascina-tion." They were the first group of individuals to become famous for being eccentric rather than for their "historically momentous achievements." The way these scientists tell it, a 1789 issue of *The Gentleman's Magazine,* which featured the obit of one Isaac Tar-rat, "a man known to hire himself out to impersonate a doctor and tell fortunes in a fur cap, a large white beard and a worn dam-ask night gown," is, at least in some small part, responsible for the rise of Kim Kardashian, she who is famous for being famous.

Of course, it wasn't until two hundred years later that the cul-ture of celebrity obsession truly exploded. Another study of obit-uaries, this time of a century's worth in the *New York Times* "notable deaths" section, found that "obits of entertainers and athletes steadily rose in rank across the 20th century, moving from seventh in 1900, to fifth in 1925, up to third in 1950 and first in 1975 and 2000, at which point they accounted for 28 percent of obits." Obituaries for religious leaders and big names in manufacturing, business, and finance fell significantly in the same time period.

Twenty-eight percent of all obituaries may not seem like much, but sociologist Patrick Nolan says this uptick is no small thing. "The magnitude of these trends is seismic," he said upon the publication of this study. "While the Greeks may have looked to their gods for guidance and entertainment, we've turned increasingly to our celebrities—entertainers and athletes." And plenty of scientists have echoed the idea that celebrity culture is basically a religion for the secularists among us. "With its myths, its rituals (the red carpet walk, the Super Bowl ring, the handprints outside Grauman's Chinese Theatre) and its ability to immortalize, it fills a similar cultural niche," journalist Carlin Flora wrote in *Psychology Today*. "In a secular society our need for ritualized idol worship can be displaced onto stars. . . . Nonreligious people tend to be more interested in celebrity culture . . . for them, celebrity fills some of the same roles the church fills for believers, like the desire to admire the powerful and the drive to fit into a community of people with shared values."

Calling it the Church of Gwyneth is even more accurate than I thought.

It's been a month since I joined said church. While the emphasis of the last month has been largely on food, I've tried to include general lifestyle tips as they've come up, just as I did with Jennifer. Some of Gwyneth's suggestions are more useful than others, but I like the idea that mastering only six dishes will be enough to bolster one-on-one dinnertime with Matt, or the suggestion that to save time, women should adopt a uniform. "I say, OK, this winter I'm going to wear minidresses and tights and this pair of jeans and these two coats," she told *Vogue* in 2008. "I wear either these Lanvin boots every day or gray Chloé ankle boots. It's like I want to eliminate all of the fuss. I don't have time anymore to sit there and be like, What should I wear? What goes with this?" Swap the minidresses for leggings, and Lanvin or Chloé for J. Crew or Gap, and I'm on board.

The goal for the month was to get control of my kitchen, which might in turn get me one step closer to feeling in control of my life. Overall, it was a success. Taking the time to create something is rewarding, and I've found I'm much more likely to sit down, take a breath, unwind, and enjoy a meal when I've spent time and energy putting it together. When Matt and I eat microwave meals, we eat in front of the TV, often separately. When I cook, we always eat at the table, together. It's a small change, but makes a big difference.

And when I sit down to a plate of pasta with homemade farmer's market pesto and slow-roasted tomatoes, or even a lunch of avocado stuffed with a Vegenaise-based dip, just the look of it makes me feel the slightest bit better about my accomplishments that day.

So while the ever-growing celebrity obsession is making me harder on myself, implementing the star-quality life changes has certainly increased my happiness. No one would look at my day-to-day and think, "Wow, she's like a celebrity!" but it's the internal uplift that I'm searching for. I've developed a step-by-step self-improvement regimen, and it's working from the inside out.

So here I am. Two months in and already conflicted—celebrity obsession is making me feel worse and better all at once. I blame Gwyneth for those thirty-six hours of cleansing misery. Yes, it was my choice to go on the detox, and no, I didn't consult my doctor as advised on Goop, but still, I'm annoyed at her in the same way I'd be annoyed at a pal who suggested a restaurant that gave me food poisoning. Not actually her fault, but . . . Still, a much bigger part of me is excited to continue on my mission. I've increased my workout routine and expanded my culinary repertoire. These are tangible self-improvements. And despite teetering on the edge of destructive celebrity obsession, there's still that research that celebrity adoration can actually increase self-esteem, so there are many plus sides to continuing on this pursuit of perfection.

And now that I'm feeling better about my body—there's a slight slimming of my figure (shrinking love handles, slightly defined abs) thanks to workouts and meals of natural food—it's time to present these improvements to the world. No one notices the hard-earned results of daily biceps curls and salad for lunch when I only ever leave the house in variations on a sweat suit.

I need to ramp up my wardrobe, and I know just the lady to help me do it.

CHAPTER THREE

SARAH JESSICA PARKER'S WARDROBE

"I would much prefer that life would allow for a beautiful shoe all day long." —Harper's Bazaar

"I don't buy anything trendy. I used to be more easily seduced by some momentary idea of what was fashionable. Now I'm slightly savvier. I still have the same ideas in my head about what looks good on me and what doesn't. I still won't wear turtlenecks." —Glamour

"I would give birth as often as I could, if I could." —Vogue

Fashion has never been my thing. I try to dress well enough, but I don't care about the fancy designers, I've never drooled over the outfits in *Vogue,* and I covet nothing from the runways of Fashion Week. I don't even know when Fashion Week is. I do have a closet full of clothes—a big closet in fact, with piles of sweaters and T-shirts and an overcrowded rack of dresses—but whenever I'm shopping with friends and one of them says, "Rachel, this is *so* you," they're usually holding a semi-stylish sweatshirt, or an otherwise fancy garment (blazer, skirt) made of sweatshirt material.

I do enjoy dressing up, getting wardrobe inspiration from *In-Style,* and shopping at local boutiques. I mean, I want to look cute in Facebook photos, of course—I'm not a monster. It's just that I can rarely muster the energy for all that, especially if I don't have a wedding, interview, or über-classy dinner date to get to. My style, when I choose to display it, is fairly casual. Leggings or jeans, tank tops, cardigans, ballet flats. But if you were to run into me on a Tuesday afternoon at my neighborhood 7-11, I'd probably be wearing an outfit that was originally intended for the gym. It's comfortable, I work from home, and it's quite possible that I got dressed early for a nighttime yoga class. There's a reason Matt calls me Sporty Spice.

I have plenty of incentives to revamp my look. Wardrobe makeovers are fun, I'm 30 and should probably dress like it, and I want to showcase the semi-toned arms I've been working so hard for. But the most important motivation is simple: my ponytail-and-fancy-sweats garb does nothing to inspire energy or happiness. It is virtually impossible to feel fabulous when you look down at your outfit and see the dressings of a sloth. I have the sense that a single change—pants with a nonelastic waistband!—could do better things for my mood than any upper I could buy at a University of New Hampshire rave.

There's science that says as much. Research suggests that while what we wear certainly influences how others see us, our outfits have an equal effect on our own attitudes and behavior. The phenomenon is called "enclothed cognition," and was best displayed in an experiment where college students were asked to wear a white coat. Those who were told it was a doctor's coat performed better on tests for attentiveness than those who thought they were wearing a painter's coat, or who didn't wear the coat at all. If you think you're in medical garb, you'll start acting like a doctor. Your attention to detail will increase. The study's authors found that the symbolic meaning of the clothes, along with the physical act of wearing them, directly affected the wearer's psychological process.

My father used to tell a story of his college roommate, who

couldn't study at night until he put on a coat and tie, similar to his high school uniform. The roommate said it made him feel like he was in "academic mode." If the enclothed cognition theory holds, the roommate probably got better grades as a result.

Scientists agree more research needs to be done on enclothed cognition. It's a fairly new field, and some researchers still say your outfit is more affected by your mood than your mood is affected by your outfit. If you feel lethargic, then your comfy, pajama-like clothes will reflect that; if you wake up with a sudden conquer-the-world vigor, you'll be more inclined to wear heels and a no-nonsense suit.

I'm a big-time believer in fake it till you make it, and enclothed cognition is its wardrobe iteration. If you want to feel happy, smile. If you want to feel fabulous, dress fabulously.

Though she is my fashion inspiration, I don't want to wear everything that Sarah Jessica Parker does. First of all, we have entirely different body types. She's a mini-human, and I'm your average pear shape. Second of all, even if I were munchkiny like her, I'm just not the type to wear a fascinator to a movie premiere. (Were I to go to a movie premiere.) Yes, she's worn some fairy-tale dresses that would be dreamy to dress up in—so much tulle!—but the SJP style moments I'm most drawn to are her on-the-street looks. Even in casual jeans and a T-shirt she looks deliberately chic, with the perfect accessories to tie it all together.

Sarah Jessica Parker is a fashion icon. It may have started with Carrie Bradshaw, but the status quickly transferred to the actress. She's an arbiter of taste, and while I may not always want to copy her exact style, I do want to copy her style philosophy. She seems like the type of gal who's confident in her getup no matter what she wears, and I want some of that for myself.

Nailing down the specifics of SJP's style philosophy should be easy. She's been profiled in every woman's magazine or celebrity TV show, she launched a reasonably priced real-woman fashion line in 2010, she briefly ran the Halston Heritage clothing line in 2011, and she seems to be BFFs with Tim Gunn, fashionisto extraordinaire. But the Sarah Jessica's Guide to Style I'm searching for is nowhere to be found. While much is made of her outfit on every red carpet or New York City street corner, she seems hesitant to tell her legions of worshippers how to dress. She rarely enumerates the must-haves or not-hots. It probably speaks well of her—she knows enough to acknowledge that her fans probably can't buy Alexander McQueen gowns, and that everyone's style is different and should be celebrated as such. She probably also knows that telling fans to imitate your choices is often received with disdain (see: Gwyneth) so she doesn't advise on what others should wear.

Lucky for me, SJP has at least provided a bit of insight into how she chooses her own looks, and I'm not too proud to take notes. Anyone who knows the names Stacy London and Clinton Kelly might already be well versed in the overall themes: Dress for your figure, embrace a great purse, find a perfect black dress, invest in well-made clothes, mix new pieces with vintage finds, and reject anything too trendy.

I've got plenty of images to pull from. Sarah Jessica Parker at a movie premiere, an awards show, on the street, with her kids—whatever scenario I'm looking for, the paparazzi have shot it. Plus, every fashion blogger and magazine out there has analyzed these pictures and come up with a style guide. Wear heels. Be a lady. Add a scarf. Make it work for your lifestyle. Accessorize even your most casual outfit.

A day spent gathering SJP tips and scouring photos makes me

want to sprint to my closet, tear off the slippers and black dance pants I got for Christmas last year (I still buy workout clothes intended for ballerinas because I still plan on being a dancer when I grow up), and slip on a pair of skinny jeans, a cool T-shirt, funky necklace, and heels. But even more than any single outfit, what I covet most is the cool confidence that emanates from all of SJP's looks. Film director Douglas McGrath put it perfectly in a 2012 issue of *Elle:* "Sarah Jessica is very glamorous in many ways, which is an exciting fantasy for many women. But unlike some style icons, where it's all cold surface beauty, she has a wonderful humanity that always shows through. She's beguiling, enchanting—and yet you never forget that she's a real person."

It's that marriage of style and humanity that I want to embody. I'm not a Hollywood starlet, so there's no reason for me to dress like I'm on the red carpet. But I'd like to liven up my everyday wear so that I'm more proud than embarrassed when I bump into a neighbor at the grocery store. Lately those run-ins end with me awkwardly apologizing: "Oh gosh, I'm such a mess. How embarrassing! I was just running to pick up toilet paper. And, look! There's some now, attached to my shoe . . ."

It's less than ideal.

I start by surveying my closet. I may not consider myself a clotheshorse, but there's a lot here. Enough that when we moved in it was pretty clear Matt would be using the closet in our second bedroom. Should this baby dream ever come true, he'll have to keep his clothes in a storage closet, but no matter. He's a boy. In fact, our bedroom closet was the first room, if you can call it a room, that sold me on the apartment where Matt and I have lived for five years. It's not exactly Cher's in *Clueless*—those rotating racks!—but it's a small walk-in and it's the biggest closet I've ever had. Fashionista or not, I'm kind of in love with it.

The first problem—and I'm sure you're shocked to hear this—is that it's a mess. I haven't done a wardrobe purge in a while, every shelf and rack is overflowing, there's a pile of clothes I'm saving for the day I shed ten pounds and another for the day I decide to deal with my hand-wash-only clothes, and the once-folded stacks of T-shirts and sweaters are now haphazard mountains.

(You know those pictures of celebrity closets that show up in fashion magazines, where they have multiple walls of shoe racks, all of which are organized first by color and then by heel height? I'm dying to know if those are real or just organized pre-photo shoot by a hired stylist. I'm guessing the latter, though I kind of want to believe the former. For aspiration's sake.)

The second problem is that my wardrobe is full of clothes I love but never wear. I mentally label items as I buy them: a going-out-on-the-town shirt, a work event blouse, a rehearsal dinner dress, fancy occasion shoes. Since I rarely go out on the town or have work events, some of my favorite items have gotten only one, if any, evening of use. It's no wonder a person doesn't feel cute and confident in her clothes when her favorite gold sparkly blouse has never left the closet. And most of my "fancy" clothes aren't even that fancy. But if it's not made of cotton or denim, I mentally file it as evening wear. A silk or satin or rayon shirt? I save those for . . . what? Dinner with SJP herself? Not gonna happen.

The paparazzi photos of Sarah Jessica pushing a stroller along the streets of Greenwich Village show her wearing casual outfits, yes, but there's usually at least a purse or pair of shoes that amp it up. Or sometimes she's walking down Park Avenue in an outfit that looks like adorable daywear on her, but is something I would save for a black-tie gala.

I've run into that before. Not with SJP of course, but I was sitting at my favorite diner, enjoying my omelet while wearing a post-workout sweat suit, and in walked a girl wearing a dress that I own, and have only ever worn to a black-tie wedding. At a diner. And she didn't look ridiculous or overdressed for a Sunday. She looked cute. A denim jacket and flats really casualize an outfit. I get that clothes can be dressed up or down, and I don't think I looked inappropriately informal at our friends' wedding, but it was an eye-opening "oh I can wear that dress more than once a year?" kind of moment.

In her book *The Happiness Project,* author Gretchen Rubin calls this "spending out." She writes: "I often found myself saving things, even when it made no sense. Like those white T-shirts I bought. I'd surmounted the challenge of buying them; then came the challenge of *wearing* them. . . . I could feel myself wanting to 'save' them in their pristine glory. But not wearing clothes is as wasteful as throwing them away." I have no problem wearing a new white T-shirt—probably until it stains badly enough that Matt refuses to be seen with me in public—but I need to "spend out" the clothes that I've relegated to fancy occasions for no logical reason.

I save clothes, I've realized, because I like to be casual during the day. I don't want to look like I'm trying too hard. But as I scan the pictures of Sarah Jessica that I've gathered for inspiration, it's clear she never looks overly done up. Confidence, and the pairing of more casual items with the higher-end stuff—a T-shirt with heels, for example—make it work. So step one of Operation: SJP is to actually wear my favorite clothes. Not for any specific occasion, but because I love them.

First up is a gray cotton bat-sleeved shirt thingie that I decided was only fit for the clubs because it has a small slit up the back. No matter that the last time I went to a club was in 2005 and even then I was that awkward girl in the corner staring at my drink and not making eye contact. Another reason I've never worn this shirt during the day is that it cost more than a cotton shirt ever should. If I spend more than $50 on something, I justify the cost by classifying it as "fancy." Shopping justification mind games are one of my specialties.

The shape of the shirt is fun—loose on top, tight around the waist—and there is absolutely no reason I should have waited this long to wear it. So this morning I pair it with burgundy jeans, nude ballet flats, and a long necklace. And then I sit down at the computer.

It's strange to be dressed up when all alone in the house. I don't look especially fancy—no one looks at me like I'm out of place when I run to the grocery store for a soda—but I'm currently sitting about ten notches higher on the fashion scale than normal. I'm typing these words wearing burgundy jeans. That is kind of trendy. Again, there's no one here to witness this change in routine. I'm writing from home, not the coffee shop where I've become known for my crop-top lululemon sweatshirt (if you thought half the material would cost only half the price, like I did, you'd be wrong). But the simple act of being dressed like someone ready, or at least willing, to face the world, actually makes me feel like I'm ready to face the world. With one simple outfit, I've tricked myself into believing I'm someone who gets up, gets dressed, and gets things done. It's amazing the difference a waistband can make.

The next week or so follows a similar pattern. Every morning I wake up, go to the gym, shower, and get dressed in my version of something cute. I've started focusing more on accessorizing. And on makeup. Nothing outrageous, but I just bought my first eye shadow in about a decade, so I've put that to use. There's no question that the whole getting ready routine takes longer now. (That pesky time issue again.) I used to pride myself on how quickly I could get out the door on any occasion. On a normal morning, I can be out of bed and out of the house—showered—in twenty minutes flat. If it's a Saturday night and I'm putting in some extra effort, forty-five minutes will do. Now I'm actually spending time considering my clothes, instead of grabbing what's most accessible. Comfort and efficiency aren't my first concerns.

I try to channel SJP and forego anything trendy in favor of something that fits and fits well. Eventually, if I want to truly embody my muse, I'll need to take some risks. Sarah Jessica is nothing if not daring on the red carpet. But for the first week, I'm happy just imitating her low-key side, and giving my wardrobe a small but decided upgrade.

It pays off fairly quickly. When I run into a friend at a party—I'm wearing leggings, boots, a blue sheer blouse layered over a black tank top, and a nude lace blazer—she tells me I look very "New York." Which I interpret to mean "city chic."

How very Sarah Jessica.

When I meet a different friend at the coffee shop for a work date, I'm wearing bright blue jeans, a gray-and-neon-green striped sweater, and ankle boots.

"Look at you," she says, with a definite hint of surprise. "You look so cute." There's confusion in her voice, too, as if she held back her next questions: "Who died? Why do you look nice?" I've gotten this same reaction from others since I've started paying better attention to what I wear. A friend of my mom's recently saw me at an engagement party, complimented my outfit, and explained, "I've only ever seen you going to and from the gym." That wasn't actually true, but I can see how my clothes made it seem as such. I decided not to correct her.

In both instances, I wanted to tell them not to sound so shocked, but the truth is, I get it. When someone has established her style as Sporty with a Hint of Hair Frizz, a change without warning can throw others off guard. I'm a bit surprised myself. My initial reaction was to be all self-deprecating about it: "This is what happens when you actually get dressed in the morning!" It was good for a laugh, and seemed to address exactly what everyone was thinking. But now I'm going a different route: a simple thank you. Jokes about my usual schlumpiness merely reinforce the idea of my gym-rat style, and I'm trying to build a Sarah Jessica Parker–inspired persona.

Even if they are the slightest bit backhanded, the compliments are welcome. Of my celebrity self-improvement categories, wardrobe is the first that others can really see. I've toned my arms and abs muscles, but my body is not exactly a Jennifer Aniston doppelgänger just yet, and the mere five pounds I've lost aren't exactly obvious when hidden under layers of clothing. The outfit upgrade is noticeable, and the compliments tell me it's working. Take yesterday afternoon. Matt came home, saw me typing away at my computer in capri jeans, the long gingham blouse I'd previously saved for date nights, and the metallic gold sneakers I bought because 1) I loved them and 2) they reminded me of an on-the-street SJP, and he asked me if I was in my fashion-inspired celebrity month.

"Yes, Sarah Jessica Parker," I said.

"You're definitely dressing better," he said. "My little fashionista."

And while I'm grateful for Matt's recognition, and the other compliments, too, it's not the outside acknowledgment that has me most excited about this month. In the past, whenever I've gotten dressed up, I've done it, at least in part, for other people. Maybe not explicitly—I rarely say, "I'm going to wear this sweater because Callie will like it"—but I often base my outfit on fitting in with my company. When I'm meeting an especially dressy friend I might wear higher heels. When I know I'm seeing a pal who only wears black, I lean toward monochromatic. The change might not be drastic, but it's there. I dress for my company. What's struck me lately is how much better I feel, internally, when I make myself presentable, even if I don't leave the house. I'm dressing well, and doing it for me rather than for anyone else.

Staying home all day is a fairly frequent occurrence in my life. Our second bedroom doubles as my workspace, and more often than not I forego even that desk for the kitchen table. I sit in our dining room–kitchen hybrid and turn it into the Rachel Bertsche Inc. command center—writing blog posts, pitching articles, answering emails. I'll run out of the house first thing for a workout or a hit of caffeine, but once I'm home, I may not leave for the rest of the day. And for a long time, on these days, I saw no reason to worry about my outfit. I wasn't going to interact with anyone, so who was I trying to impress? Why waste the time on picking out clothes when I'll probably change back into my lounge-around-the-house outfit only eight hours later?

My mother-in-law is the kind of person who dresses in a legitimate outfit every day of the year. When Matt and I visit her in Cape Cod, we'll often pass an entire day reading books, playing Scrabble, and snacking. That's literally all we'll do for the whole day. And yet Jane will emerge from her bedroom in full garb. Nothing fancy, but jeans, a tucked in blouse, boots, jewelry. For years I've wondered about this. *It's just us!* I think. *Doesn't she want to be comfortable? Who is she dressing for? What a waste.* But now I get it. Looking down at myself and feeling presentable does wonders for my mood. It gives me confidence. It helps me feel ready to tackle a project—there's that enclothed cognition again. And this can be especially helpful for my work-from-home life-style. Dressing like I'm going to bed makes me feel like I should be going to bed. Dressing like I'm at work gives me the extra motivation to actually do work. So instead of dressing for others—making myself presentable because I have to do errands or go to a meeting or dine with friends—I dress for myself. I put on a fa-vorite pair of ballet flats, or take five extra minutes to do makeup, or put on a necklace just because. I feel better—happier—afterward, and it's hard to feel like you're rocking your whole life when you're wearing a sweat-stained T-shirt and ratty pants. It just is.

I've been humming along—working out, cooking, putting my favorite closet items to use—for a week when I get another monthly sign that I'm still not pregnant. It's horribly dishearten-ing, even depressing, and serves as a repeated reminder that the thing I want most is the one thing I can't control, no matter how hard I try or how many celebrities I imitate, and it's enough to send me back into pajama pants for at least today.

As it happens, Sarah Jessica Parker has gone through a similar struggle—she said as much to *Vogue* in 2010, when discussing the twin daughters she and husband Matthew Broderick had via sur-rogate. "[We] tried and tried and tried and tried and tried to get pregnant, but it just was not to be, the conventional way—I would give birth as often as I could, if I could." I'm not exactly comforted by this information (while I may be using these celeb-rities as self-improvement inspiration, I haven't drunk enough of the Kool-Aid to confuse a magazine interview with a heart-to-heart with a friend), but there is something to knowing you aren't alone. I haven't shared my fertility issues with a lot of people, so I don't have many women to commiserate with. These words from SJP make me feel as if pregnancy is the great leveler. Natural conception isn't something you can buy or get special treatment for, no matter how famous you are.

There is something reassuring about the idea that this is one area where it doesn't matter who you are or who you know.

Celebrity pregnancies—or pregnancy struggles—are chronicled by the tabloids to an almost freakish degree. Three pounds gained, or an especially loose shirt, is clearly a sign that a star is with child. Every celebrity I've chosen as inspiration—Jennifer, Gwyneth, SJP, and also Tina Fey, Jennifer Garner, and Julia Roberts—has probably read national news reports about her own attempts to bear children. Perhaps this should make me feel a bit better. Infertility has become a tad less taboo, if only because of Giuliana Rancic and Khloé Kardashian's televised struggles to get pregnant. Sarah Jessica has spoken publicly about her fertility problems, and so have Celine Dion, Courteney Cox, Nicole Kidman, Marcia Cross, Brooke Shields, Angela Bassett, Emma Thompson, and Sherri Shepherd. But ultimately, of course, other people's problems don't make me feel better about my own. I wish we could all get knocked up right when we wanted to, celebrity or not.

Two months ago, after a trip to his office for bloodwork, my OB-GYN gave me his email address and told me we should "regroup" in a couple of months if I was still not pregnant. Those months have passed. In fact, Matt and I have been trying now for nine months. Couples our age are usually instructed to wait a year before doing major fertility testing, so I don't know if it's because my doctor can sense my desperation, or because some experts in the field are leaning toward taking action earlier than the traditional year mark, but during our virtual regroup, my doctor suggests Matt get a semen analysis as a starting point. It's a relatively easy and inexpensive fertility test compared with the tests for women, and we already know from previous blood tests that I'm at least ovulating. This is a reasonable first step.

It's increasingly evident as I pursue my celeb-style life that what I crave is control. I started this experiment because I was feeling like a hot mess. Or, if the sweat suit perma-outfit was any indication, maybe just a mess. I saw pictures of celebrities in magazines, and even sometimes regular women on the street, who projected an aura of having it all together—that certain brand of confidence that radiates from head to toe—and I wanted it for myself. It would come from conquering my life instead of letting my life conquer me. Or something like that. So I embarked on my celebrity-inspired quest with the express intention that if I did what Jennifer or Gwyneth or Sarah Jessica did, and achieved the level of confidence and class that *People* leads us to believe they have in bucketloads, I would feel less harried, more in control and, in the end, happier. And so far, there are days where I absolutely feel this is the case. But on days like today, when the baby I yearn for seems completely out of my reach, it's hard not to feel derailed. Because no matter how much control I have over my day-to-day appearance or energy level, I can't control pregnancy. I can pee on a stick every morning, or tumble into the void of the obsessive online pregnancy message boards, or overanalyze every yawn—"is this average fatigue? Or pregnancy exhaustion?"—but in the end it's going to happen or it's not, and right now it seems that it's not. And yes, I know it's only been nine months, which in the grand scheme of things is hardly forever, and I'm aware that plenty of couples try for years, but when you're in the thick of it, those three quarters of a year feel like an eternity.

I allow myself one day a month to wallow. There are tears and feelings of hopelessness and a potentially melodramatic call to Matt regarding how we'll never have kids. He is, as always, totally levelheaded about this pursuit.

"I just want a baby," I say. "I want our little baby."

"We'll get our family," Matt says. "This sucks, but we'll figure it out."

So much for enclothed cognition. Even the world's cutest outfit couldn't lift my spirits right now. I'm feeling crappy, and my wardrobe follows suit. In my favorite sweatpants and old T-shirt, I take my place on the couch, order my pad thai, turn on *SVU,* and settle in.

* * *

A day later, with my pity party wrapped up, it's time to take these SJP efforts up a notch. So far, she's inspired me to get dressed in the morning and to put some effort into looking nice, even if I'm only running errands. That doesn't mean looking unnecessarily fancy for a trip to the deli, but merely paying attention rather than throwing on the first sweatshirt and Uggs I can find. To really embrace Sarah Jessica's style is to push fashion a bit further. To be a little daring, and still have fun with it.

Sarah Jessica claims not to have Carrie Bradshaw levels of fashion obsession. She says she doesn't understand being labeled a style icon herself, and claims that the odds of her looking not presentable when leaving the house in the morning are "pretty high." Yet when it comes to getting dressed up, Sarah Jessica gives Carrie a run for her money. In *Tim Gunn's Guide to Style,* Gunn lumps SJP with fashionistas Chloë Sevigny and Kate Moss, labeling them "the risk takers." He goes on to explain their signature look: "We can admire, but we cannot endorse. The risk-taker approach is simply too risky for a layperson."

I am most definitely a fashion layperson. Perhaps I should have chosen someone more stylistically accessible, like Natalie Portman, whom Gunn says is fairly easy to imitate since "the key to [her] look is simplicity," and she is "rarely seen in a heel." But for now it's go big or go home. I'm taking on the stars whose names are synonymous with a lifestyle—be it fitness or food or fashion. They are the walking representations of what we want to be. Natalie Portman is not synonymous with fashion and style, despite her good taste. Sarah Jessica Parker is.

After his warning against imitating the likes of SJP, Tim Gunn adds a caveat: "One big or striking fashion item, if worn in isolation, is permissible. . . . But dipping the toes into the crystalline waters of risk must be a slow process. Which means, if you're wearing the antler hat, you must leave the caribou vest at home."

What I need, clearly, is a striking fashion item.

This is another one of those moments where the financial constraints of being a mere mortal might be in direct conflict with my goals of being fabulous. The most glamorous of striking fashion items are usually priced accordingly.

"How do you feel about me spending a fortune on a statement piece?" I ask Matt.

"I have absolutely no idea what you are talking about." We're on the phone, and he's in the office, apparently too busy to discuss the merits of buying an SJP-style fur vest.

"Sometimes to live like a celebrity you need to spend a little money," I explain. "In order to really embody Sarah Jessica

Parker, I need to wear something that is bold and maybe crazy, but that I love. So I was thinking I'd go shopping for something like that."

"Can't you find something bold and crazy *without* spending a fortune?" Matt asks.

"You're no fun," I say. "But maybe."

The clothing boutique on my corner has high-end clothes for high-end prices, and I tend to love everything in the store, so I go straight there after hanging up with Matt. I'm not sure exactly what I'm looking for, but I figure I'll know it when I see it. Tim Gunn sent visions of fur vests dancing in my head, but I'm thinking anything outside my usual wardrobe box will do. The racks are filled with beautiful tops and dresses that I'd certainly make mine if money were no object—oh, the plight of not actually being a star!—but no single piece that would add a wow factor to every outfit.

I've spent way too much time in this store over the past five years, but as a result I've become friendly with Lauren, the manager, who has impeccable taste in clothes. She knows my general style, so as I sift through the racks, she asks if there's anything specific I'm looking for.

"Actually, I'm in the market for a bold signature item, like something Sarah Jessica Parker would wear," I explain. Lauren looks surprised and I don't blame her. The items I've purchased from her store are usually more classic, investment pieces—a timeless little black dress or a cashmere sweater—for which the cost seems less extravagant in relation to the years of use I will get out of it. The store has a few bold pieces, but nothing that feels especially me.

"Are you trying to dress more like her?" Lauren asks.

"I am," I say. "Or I guess I'm trying to inhabit her style philosophy. Which, according to Tim Gunn's book, means wearing a risky statement piece if you really, really love it."

Lauren laughs, perhaps because she's fashion savvy enough to have her own style, rather than borrowing someone else's. But one benefit of mooching the habits of a mentor—be it SJP's clothing choices or Gwyneth's cooking—is that it forces you to start somewhere. Most great artists begin by copying someone else's work before developing their own technique, and while less high-brow, this is no different. I need a jumping-off point. I don't expect to spend the rest of my life cooking only from Gwyneth's cookbook or exclusively following Jennifer's workout plan, but you've got to start somewhere.

And that's when I remember.

"Actually, I do have one kind of crazy item that I would absolutely love to wear, if only I knew how," I tell Lauren. "And I guess it's very Sarah Jessica."

She looks at me expectantly.

"It's a tutu," I say. "A purple tutu."

The story of the tutu is bizarre and amazing. I have spent my entire life not-so-secretly wishing I was a dancer. I love my job, but if I had unlimited talent and access, I'd be a ballerina. Maybe a ballerina with a hip-hop-dancing side gig. Unfortunately, my pirouettes peaked in seventh grade, so now I satisfy my dancer dreams with cardio hip-hop classes, ballerina art—there are pictures of dancers all around my apartment—and the aforementioned love affair with ballet flats. Then, last year, I was perusing the trendy exercise clothing store lululemon when I came upon the most amazing tutu. It came in deep purple or black. It was short, and went straight out from the waist. This wasn't a bunch of tulle that could double as a skirt, it was a legit dance class tutu.

It would be perfect over a leotard and tights, paired with pointe shoes. The shape was classic while the dark colors made it very *Black Swan*.

I had absolutely no use for it, and I wanted it. Badly.

Given the $98 price point, I never bought the tutu. I visited it, showing it to friends and explaining that this was the tutu of my dreams, but I could find no excuse to spend $98 on something I'd have occasion to wear only when twirling around my own living room.

A couple of months later a friend and I drove an hour outside the city to wait in line for the first ever lululemon warehouse sale. We were told it would be a collection of all our favorite clothes for up to 80 percent off. The line to get in was an hour long, and lululemon staff was on hand to entertain suckers like us who gave up an entire day just to buy a cheaper pair of leggings.

That entertainment involved various contests. Contests for which the prize was a tutu.

Apparently, even at discount prices, people don't spend money on tutus. No huge surprise—even when I fell in love with it I couldn't figure out how they were going to move that product. But now that I could get the tutu for free I was determined to own it, so I entered a plank contest, which involved getting on the floor of the warehouse and holding the top of a pushup position for longer than any of my competitors. In the end I didn't really outlast anyone—the judges called it after three minutes passed since almost everyone was still planking. But that worked for me. *You get a tutu! You get a tutu! Everybody gets a tutuuuuuuuuuuu!*

So for the past year, I've had a purple tutu in my closet, though it doesn't see much action. I've worn it once. Some friends and I went ice skating and I figured if I couldn't be a ballerina I might as well be a figure skater. I got plenty of compliments from fellow skaters that day, but I'm still not sure if they were genuine accolades, or the kind of comments that come when someone is wearing something so outrageous that you stare for too long and suddenly realize you have to say something. And so you say "What a cool tutu!" when what you really mean is "What the hell are you wearing?"

All this to say: I have a tutu. It's the perfect out-there item with which I can dabble in high fashion, or at least risk-taker fashion.

"It's not like a tulle skirt," I tell Lauren. "It's a tutu. It doesn't cover my butt at all, so I'd have to wear leggings under it. But I'm sort of obsessed with it."

Lauren thinks a tutu is very doable, especially one that isn't pink. She has a petticoat she wears under a long sweater or jacket, she says, so the tulle is just barely sticking out from underneath. "If you contrast it with something more masculine—like one of Matt's old sweaters—it could totally work."

At home, I do some experimenting. I try it with a gray V-neck cashmere sweater that used to be my dad's. Lauren was right, the oversized boyfriend-style works perfectly with the tutu. So does a chunky cable-knit sweater that I once bought at her store. The key, as she said, is to make the tutu barely there, and to not pair it with anything else too precious.

I'm determined to wear the getup in public, but I'm also nervous. I'm glad Sarah Jessica has upgraded my wardrobe choices overall, but I don't want to look like a clown. Still, part of fashion is having fun with it, and SJP embodies that more than anyone. She always seems to enjoy what she's wearing, and so should I.

When I tell a friend that I want to wear my tutu once a week or so, she laughs and tells me I should implement Tutu Tuesdays. And though I'm pretty sure she's joking, I think it's brilliant. Tutu Tuesdays are just the fashion pick-me-up I need.

And so on the following Tuesday, I get dressed in my preapproved outfit. Black leggings, black wool sweater, and tutu. There are no special occasions today—my tutu sees the outdoors only when I go for a walk to the grocery store and another walk to a coffee shop, and later when I meet a potential new friend for dinner. We've met only once, about ten years ago, and I've resigned myself to the fact that she'll probably think me crazy when I show up to a low-key sushi restaurant in a purple tutu, but like everyone else I've encountered today, she doesn't even notice.

I shouldn't be surprised. One thing I've learned over the years is that no one is paying as much attention to me as I think they are. While I might feel awkward asking a new acquaintance out to lunch, chances are she's not analyzing my approach. When I'm convinced my three extra holiday pounds are glaringly obvious, everyone else is probably too busy lamenting over their own weight to notice mine. And when it comes to my clothes, I am almost definitely scrutinizing my outfit more than anyone else is.

This isn't the case for celebrities, of course. In their line of work, everyone—casting directors, magazine editors, fans—really is assessing and judging. And perhaps that's why they appear so perfect. They have to. Whether or not it's fair or healthy or even sane, we're the ones devouring articles about the stars, aspiring to be like them when they appear flawless and paying even closer attention when they don't. Despite my endeavor to be more like various celebrities, I don't envy that.

It's another conundrum of the perfection complex that so many of us women have developed: We consume media about celebrities, and because they appear so fabulous, we want to, too.

But perhaps they only appear so fabulous because they know they're being watched. If no cameras followed Jennifer Aniston around 24/7, if getting lead movie roles didn't require super-model looks, would she still work so hard to look so good? I can't know for sure, but it's hard to imagine.

In that sense, it's plenty more pleasant to be a regular Jane. No one is evaluating me as harshly as I am evaluating myself. And with this tutu, I may feel a bit silly, but here's the truth: Every time I look down and see that bundle of tulle sticking out from under my sweater, I get a rush. I feel like a little girl playing dress-up.

It's an unlikely source of such a high, but if I can find happiness in a purple tutu, I should probably embrace it.

After the tutu success, I stop into Lauren's store to show her the photographic evidence of her fashion mastery. We get to talking about the scarf she's wearing, and how I never can figure out how to tie mine, so she gives me an impromptu lesson.

During this wardrobe how-to, it occurs to me that Lauren has become the closest thing I can find to a stylist.

Just as most celebrities have fitness trainers who whip their butts into shape, they also largely have stylists who help them choose outfits for the red carpet and other appearances. When obsessing over the impeccable looks of a favorite star, it's easy to forget how much help she probably gets. And it's not just in the looks department. Nannies, chefs, and assistants are all often on the payroll. In a Forbes.com article about celebrity nannies, enti-tled "Hollywood's Dirtiest Little Secret," author Kiri Blakeley writes: "Who could blame women for being awestruck at these celebrity moms who, somehow, manage to keep their children clean, well-behaved and fashionable, while they also maintain glamorous careers, travel the world, always look fabulous and well-toned, and, oh yeah, still keep a hot, successful husband (Brad Pitt! Tom Cruise!) happy? Who could blame regular women for beating themselves up for not living up to this ideal? . . . What we don't see are the armies behind the scenes who make this scenario possible."

We also don't see when these supposedly happy celebs aren't so happy after all—like Blakeley's Tom Cruise example. Sure we thought he and Katie had it all. Until they broke up.

While some celebrity "helpers" have become well known in their own right—trainer Tracy Anderson or superstylist Rachel Zoe, for example—it's true that most are kept under wraps. When you see a picture of Angelina Jolie traveling with her kids, you rarely see any of her supposed twenty-five staff members, which reportedly include nannies, doctors, and nurses. Celebrities who are photographed running from one meeting to another rarely credit their assistants for coordinating their schedules, and photo spreads of Mariah Carey or Rachel Bilson in their organized fashion-filled closets never include the stylist or housekeeper who is very likely responsible for keeping the shelves looking so pristine.

And this is probably the question I'm asked most often when friends or family inquire about my current quest for celebrity fabulousness: What about all their help?

In our celeb-savvy society, while we might not see the legions of trainers or nannies or assistants or stylists in the pages of *Us Weekly*, we know they're there. The cat's out of the bag. We also know that these perks don't come cheap.

I have no one on my payroll. No trainer. No chef. No stylist. And yet, I've learned there are ways to get help. You can barter for services, as I do at my gym where I still watch kids or sit at the front desk on a weekly basis. Or, even better, you can make friends with the right people.

When it comes to getting style advice, especially, befriending employees at stores you love goes a long way. Here's a little secret: People love sharing their expertise. Let them know you respect their opinion and insight, and they're pretty generous with all that know-how. And if you're a loyal client, even better. Suddenly, you might be the first to hear when new stock is in, or when the sweater you've been coveting goes on sale. And if you need advice on how to make a favorite piece of clothing (say, a tutu) work, you've got your go-to.

It might not be Rachel Zoe pulling just-for-you looks from Oscar de la Renta's runway show, but it's the next best thing.

All this SJPing, mixed with my Jennifer and Gwyneth regimens, has gone to my head. I'm enjoying the fruits of my labor so far—more muscles, less takeout, many more cute outfits—but it has come at a price. I've hit my vanity peak. Seriously. I've turned into one of those girls who can't pass a mirror, not even a window, without staring at her reflection. Are my legs improving? Is my outfit cute from all angles? I've gotten into the habit of taking pictures of myself in the mirror with my phone. A lot. I guess this isn't so outrageous given the Instagram-obsessed world we live in. In Mindy Kaling's book *Is Everyone Hanging Out Without Me? (And Other Concerns)* she writes an entire essay about her tendency to take selfies. "My BlackBerry photos . . . make me laugh. They are all horribly, horribly narcissistic. My BlackBerry camera has proven to exist primarily as a mirror to see if my makeup came out okay."

I've always believed Mindy and I could be best friends. (This is not an original thought. Pretty much every woman I know has this same hunch about herself and Ms. Kaling.) The passion for fad diets, celebrity photos, and rom-coms? She's totally inside my head. And while her obsession with cellphone photos of herself is laughable and endearing, mine is just sort of pathetic. I'm glad I don't dress like someone who doesn't care anymore, but every now and then I miss not caring. It took a lot less energy.

At the end of the day, it's about balance. I'm glad I'm putting some concerted effort into the areas of my life that some might call superficial, but I don't want to run the risk of letting fashion and fitness take over my brain space entirely. I'd like the appearance of my arm muscles to occupy a slightly smaller percentage of my daily thoughts, not to mention the fact that I need to redouble my focus on what actually brings in the money to retain this celebrity-imitating existence: work.

When I told Lauren during my last visit that I worried my new Sarah Jessica Parker obsession was making me ever more vain, she nodded in understanding.

"Whenever I go to business lunches, all we talk about is shopping," she said. "It's my industry, and even I want to think about something else sometimes." Like she said, it's her industry. It's not mine. I need to come back to earth.

To her credit, Sarah Jessica Parker is not out there saying women should try to emulate her wardrobe or her looks. In fact, she has very clearly stated the opposite. "My job requires me to put on a little dress and run around the streets of New York in heels," she told Oprah toward the end of her *Sex and the City* days. "But I also had the financial means to hire a yoga teacher to come to my house while my sitter watched the newborn. For 95 percent of women, that's not realistic. So when I hear that people are discussing how this actress got skinny, I say, 'Who gives a crap how she got in shape?' We should find other role models."

Part of me wants to raise a fist in support. We *should* have better role models! Woman power! The other part of me thinks: Sure, that's easy for Sarah Jessica Parker to say. She's Sarah Jessica Parker.

But I do need to move on to other sources of inspiration. Or at least add a new one to the batch. For my sanity, and also for my wallet. Fashion and gourmet food and fitness DVDs and gym memberships are expensive. Not as expensive as private chefs and personal stylists, but not free. If I want to continue to afford them, I need to get back to some serious work. In regards to all these celebrities, while they may be revered for their bodies or fashion or entertaining prowess, it should be recognized that they are all extremely hard workers and good businesswomen. They wouldn't be so successful otherwise. But if there is one woman whose work ethic I admire above all else, it would be that other fan favorite "we could totally be BFFs" funnywoman.

Tina Fey, of course.

CHAPTER FOUR

TINA FEY'S WORK ETHIC

"After each fourteen-hour acting class was over, I would meet up with five or six writers at my apartment to catch up on what they had written during the day. During those early days we'd order food and work until one or two in the morning.... I would excuse myself occasionally to change a diaper in the night.... One night I put my daughter to bed, worked with the writers all night, and in the morning when she toddled out, the writers were still there. It was the best worst thing ever."

—*Bossypants*

"While it would be great to work out an hour a day, there is something inherently sort of selfish about it. I can't do it." —*Harper's Bazaar*

"I feel like I represent normalcy in some way. What are your choices today in entertainment? People either represent youth, power or sexuality. And then there's me, carrying normalcy." —*Vogue*

I know I'm in the company of pretty much every woman in America when I declare my girl crush on Tina Fey. What's interesting about the Tina craze, though, is that we all seem to adore her for the exact opposite reasons that we do the Jennifers and Gwyneths of the world. If we want to be Jen because she's a more perfect version of ourselves, and we adore Gwyn because she's straight-up flawless and does everything right while never breaking a sweat (except when she's supposed to be sweating, and even then it's more of a sheen), then we want to befriend Tina because we think she actually *is* like us, seemingly down-to-earth and well adjusted and relatively normal-looking. She's perfectly imperfect. *Salon* describes her as "a regular gal you could easily imagine eating nachos with in your sweatpants." *Rolling Stone* claims she is hero-worshipped, at least in part, for her "cerebral, hyperwordy brand of humor, and her megafunctional geek-overdog personality." And author Curtis Sittenfeld seems to speak for all of us when she writes in *The New York Times* that, "This is the magic of Tina Fey: With her brown hair and her glasses and her nice-seeming husband who's shorter than she is, she seems like one of us, like me or my friends or my sisters (as my sister, Jo, put it in an e-mail, 'I love her because she's like me but funnier'), at the same time that she's ridiculously successful and famous. And on top of that, she's just how we'd want to be, just how we'd imagine ourselves, if we *were* ridiculously successful and famous."

That's an important point, of course. Tina Fey isn't actually your average Jane. She is, indeed, ridiculously successful and famous. *The Hollywood Reporter* named her the most powerful actress of 2012. She is a movie star, a TV star, and she tosses her hair around with the best of them in that Garnier Fructis commercial for golden-brown hair dye.

The one thing we are constantly reminded of when it comes to Tina—and not in an in-your-face way, but in a you-deserve-all-the-success-that's-come-to-you way—is how hard she's worked for everything she's achieved. Before we fell in love with her, and those glasses, on *Saturday Night Live*'s "Weekend Update," she was the show's head writer. She wrote the cult hit *Mean Girls,* created *30 Rock,* and penned *Bossypants.* She's not just a pretty face or funny lady (though she is both), but she's damn smart.

And since anyone who admires Tina or *30 Rock* knows that Liz Lemon is a frazzled, fifteen-years-ago version of the real-life star, we get a sense of how much work it takes to do what she does.

Writers, especially, seem to bow down to Ms. Fey. Eric Spitznagel at *The Believer,* a literary magazine founded by author and publisher Dave Eggers, pinpointed this extra-enthusiastic fan base back in 2003, even before *Mean Girls* or *30 Rock* or *Bossypants:* "Writers love Tina Fey because she's living proof of our own potential. When she was hired as a co-anchor for *SNL*'s 'Weekend Update,' and even more surprisingly, became an overnight celebrity because of it, comedy writers everywhere took notice. Her improbable stardom confirms our suspicions that if we were only given a chance in the spotlight, we would prove once and for all that we are exactly as attractive and witty as we always suspected. Not many writers are as charming in person as they are on the page. But Tina has proven that we, in our dreams, are not entirely deluded."

I'm not a comedy writer, but her influence on all of us who try to make a go of putting words on the page is the same. Tina Fey has single-handedly led me to believe that if only I worked as hard as she does, I too could be that successful. Or close.

So the theme for this month, in essence, is simple: Work my ass off. Channel Tina, write brilliant words, and realize my career dreams.

There are a few minor issues with this plan. The main one is that, realistically, I'm not going to have Tina levels of achievement. I'm just not. Most of us won't. I don't even know if I would necessarily want her life. But the idea is that if I emulate her interminable work ethic, I could conquer my own career goals. I'd be a television critic! I'd pen regular features for all the magazines I've been meaning to pitch but instead just read on the toilet! More and more opportunities would come my way, and—best of all—I'd love every minute of it! Even working until 1 A.M.!

The whole "loving every minute of it" part is where the biggest hiccup comes in. While I wouldn't say I love exercising, I don't dread it, either. Cooking is fun, even if I haven't been as steadfast as I'd like in my nightly Gwyneth meals. And I get a girly pleasure in futzing over my wardrobe. The previous elements of this quest have been, overall, enjoyable. And while I like working—I'd rather have this job than any other—like anyone, I'd rather be on vacation. The act of sitting down at my computer doesn't get me excited. It's like Dorothy Parker said: "I hate writing, I love having written." So I certainly don't know that I like working enough to work as hard as Tina.

When I tell a friend that I am harnessing my current celebrity-inspired efforts to imitate Tina Fey's work ethic, she asks me what that entails.

"So far I think it just means writing. All the time," I say. "With every free moment."

"That's what I don't get about overachievers like her," my friend says. "When I get home from a day at the office, I need at least ninety minutes to decompress. I just lay there on the couch. I veg. Doesn't Tina Fey ever veg?"

"I don't think so," I say. "Not according to *Bossypants*. I'm pretty sure all she does is work, or hang out with her daughters. As much as I love her, I don't think I'll love living like her."

The whole plan—write, write, write some more, and don't waste too much time sleeping—sounds exhausting, and I'm not even forced to juggle the whole motherhood thing with my constant work. Nor do I have a staff of three hundred people on a sitcom of my creation counting on me to show up to the set and generate paychecks each week. The demands on my career and home life are dramatically lesser than Tina's and I'm tired just thinking about keeping up with her. I wonder when she last felt rested.

What I need to do is figure out some specific work-ethic-related, Tina-inspired goals. "Work always" is too nebulous.

I draw up guidelines:

1. **Bring writing notebook with me at all times. Scribble ideas, or draft assignments, whenever I'm caught with a free moment.** This is, after all, how Tina wrote *Bossypants*. "I started carrying a notebook around the set of *Date Night*," she told *Entertainment Weekly*. "[Director] Shawn Levy was making fun of me: 'You're trying to write your book right *now?*' 'Yeah, I'm trying to write it on turnarounds. I bought a composition book and everything!'"

2. **Stop thinking I need a long stretch of uninterrupted time in order to get anything done.** In that same *EW* interview, the writer-producer-mom explained the process of writing one of the most beloved chapters of *Bossypants*, "The Mother's Prayer for Its Daughter." Says Tina: "It was a Saturday morning and I said to [my husband] Jeff, 'I'll go downstairs to the lobby—I'll just try to write for an hour, and then we can all go out to have our day.'"

3. **Get over the idea of separating work life and personal life.** The benefit of working from home and working for myself is that I can do my work anywhere, at any time. Yet when I started this phase of my career, I was determined to make it a Monday through Friday, nine-to-five gig, and to keep my work self separate from my personal self. But if you want to work as hard as Tina Fey, you've got to be willing to give late nights, or weekend mornings, to the cause.

The general summary of these rules isn't unlike my initial assumption: Working like Tina Fey just means working all the time. But they may help give me the kick in the pants I need to remotivate my writing. Because as it turns out, it's easy to get used to a lifestyle focused mainly on exercise, cooking, and dressing up. I need to bring that same spring to my work step. And since I chose this career because I wanted to do what I love, I need to reignite the spark.

And so I try. I bring my computer to the coffee shop early on a Saturday morning to get some writing done before kicking off the weekend. I type notes into my iPhone when ideas strike at a restaurant or a stoplight. I'm not sure I'm conquering much more in terms of sheer pages produced or projects finished, but having the spirit of Tina as my guide makes me feel more purposeful.

* * *

It's an unseasonably warm evening for September, so I decide to walk the thirty minutes to the restaurant where I'm meeting a friend for dinner. While the reason for walking was more SJP than Tina (I don't particularly believe Sarah Jessica's claims that she stays thin by walking around Manhattan, but that doesn't mean I'm too good to try it myself), I've found that giving my mind uninterrupted time to wander is an especially effective way to generate creativity. It's on walks—or runs, or long car drives, or leisurely showers—where I come up with most of my ideas worth pursuing. Staring at a computer screen and occasionally gazing out the window, though it looks so glamorously literary on *Sex and the City*, doesn't generate much imagination. I tried to capitalize on the whole walking-as-brainstorming realization by creating a treadmill desk once, but when I nearly dropped my computer off the kitchen-tray-turned-workspace I'd so brilliantly MacGyvered, I thought better of it.

It was on this long walk when another magazine assignment began to write itself. And, holy Tina, I actually had my notebook! By the time my friend arrived at the sushi joint, I'd already scribbled three pages.

"You look like a real journalist," she said when she walked in to find me scrunched over my notebook. I felt ridiculous—*really? You need to show the world you're a writer by furiously hand-writing in a restaurant? How Hemingway*—but also accomplished. I'd just written a quick five hundred words, after all, which on a random Monday morning during a less Tinafied moment could take me more than an hour. (Words move slowly when the process looks something like, write one sentence, check Facebook, email, and EntertainmentWeekly.com, write another sentence, scroll Instagram, repeat . . .)

This is how *Bossypants* happened, people. One scribble at a time.

* * *

A week later, Matt and I meet for lunch after his first appointment with a urologist. The semen analysis ordered by my doctor, and then a second one, both determined that at least part of our baby-making problem has been due to "male factor infertility," so he suggested Matt see a specialist.

"He said we could keep trying for another couple of months," Matt tells me, "but that while most couples have a 30 percent chance of getting pregnant in any given month, ours is closer to 5 or 10 percent."

This news isn't great, but isn't totally unexpected. And while the prognosis seems grim, I am strangely comforted. The most frustrating aspect of the last ten months has been the lack of control. Or answers. Or solutions. My OB-GYN originally told me to be patient—that 90 percent of thirty-year-olds get pregnant within one year, and that most don't succeed in the first three months. I've been reminding myself of these statistics every month, but they provide less and less comfort as time goes by. Every time I hear of another friend who's expecting, I feel a pang of bitter jealousy that in turn makes me feel guilty. I don't want to be the grumpy friend who can't celebrate someone else's good news. I want to be a bundle of unbridled enthusiasm. And while I can, and do, smile and squeal with the best of them on the outside, inside my uterus is pouting like the kid picked last for the kickball team.

By the time Matt went in for his analysis, I was convinced something was up. I try not to be impatient and freak out prematurely, creating problems where there are none, but after ten months of tracking, reading fertility books (with both welcome advice—*eat full-fat dairy!*—and the gross kind—*feel for your cervical mucus!*), and taking pregnancy tests that always come up negative, I was ready to admit defeat. A baby felt out of my reach, and with every piece of well-intentioned but unsolicited advice— "Just stop stressing and it will happen," "You need to abandon all the tracking and create a romantic evening," "It's all about relaxing and being spontaneous"—I got that much closer to punching the well-meaning know-it-all in the face.

Since 90 percent of the time that know-it-all was my mom, this seemed like a bad idea.

An actual infertility diagnosis, while certainly not ideal and a bit of a punch in the gut, at least provides some answers. We have a real, documentable problem. And where there are problems, there may be solutions. The news meant we could move forward with knowledge. We could take action. There was something to fix. There was control.

At least a little bit.

"Assuming nothing happens for the next couple of months, the doctor suggested IVF," Matt says. "He says IUI wouldn't work for us, and that given our age and your clean bill of health, we're good IVF candidates."

From the limited infertility research I've allowed myself thus far, I know that IVF, or in vitro fertilization, involves taking the woman's egg and fertilizing it with the man's sperm outside of the womb. I know it would mean a number of self-administered hormone injections, and that it ups the chances of twins. I also know it's expensive.

IUI, or intrauterine insemination, on the other hand, is a less invasive, less expensive procedure. According to the American Pregnancy Association, "IUI is a fertility treatment that uses a catheter to place a number of washed sperm directly into the uterus." The point is to eliminate some of the work for the sperm and to increase the number of them that reach the fallopian tubes, thereby increasing your pregnancy chances.

Originally, my OB-GYN thought IUI would be our next step. Now it seems as if we're going to skip it all together, and that's fine with me. I just want to get the baby train moving.

"If he thinks we're going to need IVF, why should we try for a couple more months?" I ask. "Why not just get started?"

"I think he wants us to finish out the official year," Matt says. "But I had the same question."

We're silent as we both contemplate the same thing: Is it time to take this baby quest up a notch? Or are we jumping the gun? We don't want to act too quickly out of sheer impatience (if I'm the type to move hastily on any decision, Matt is my opposite, taking forever to mull over even what to order for dinner), but we don't want to sit around waiting for no reason, either. I didn't have specific expectations for how Matt's appointment would turn out, but I guess part of me thought this doctor would prescribe a magic pill or one easy lifestyle change (colder showers? looser boxers?) and that would be that. The reality that we could be another couple seeking infertility treatment, and soon, seems to be settling in at this lunch.

I spend the next couple of days processing Matt's news. The more I think about it, the more I realize I'd rather start the IVF process immediately than wait another two months on the 5 to 10 percent chance that the stars align for us. Had I been confronted with this same dilemma four months ago, I'm not sure I would have felt the same way. Before this quest, I was the queen of inertia. I felt almost plagued by lethargy and a general idea of all the things I could, or *should*, be doing, if only I had a bit more energy or motivation. Maybe it was working from home and the resulting absence of daily social interaction. Maybe it was a lack of excitement for the projects I had in the works and the frustration with the whole baby quest. Or maybe it was sheer burnout from a couple of nonstop years of working two jobs and running on overdrive as I tried to build a marriage, career, and social life in Chicago. Most likely it was a combo platter of all three, but a part of me thinks I would have been much more bummed, and less go-get-'em, about this new challenge before this celebrity-inspired self-improvement quest began. That's not to say that cooking more or dressing better is the key to tackling infertility, but that taking a more deliberate and proactive stand in one area of your life begets another, and now I feel more empowered to attack the issues head-on.

When it comes to motherhood, Tina Fey has a lot to say, and it's interesting to read her take on the mommying job as I contemplate my own future. Despite the whole not-being-pregnant thing, I can't stop myself from considering how I'll proceed with the work-life balance issue if and when I do have a child. It's a hard dilemma to avoid when articles like *The Atlantic*'s "Why Women Still Can't Have It All"—complete with a baby in a briefcase—and Sheryl Sandburg's bestselling *Lean In* make national news. Ever since I've started working for myself, people have told me how lucky I am to have a job that affords me the ability to work *and* be at home with a child one day. It's true that I'm lucky to have flexibility and control over my own schedule. It's not true, however, that I'll be able to sit at home and take care of a baby while simultaneously tackling assignments and trying to meet deadlines. My dream is to figure out a plan that allows me more-than-average time at home with a child, but also enough hours alone to get adequate work done.

Spoken like a woman with zero children.

In navigating the whole career-versus-mothering question, I'd be smart to take a cue from Ms. Fey. She has two daughters, and still works harder than any woman I'll ever know. The best part about her working motherhood isn't that she successfully juggles parenting and a more traditional job, but that she has been fairly honest about how tough it is to try to do it all. In *Bossypants,* Tina doesn't sugarcoat her reality: "I would tell myself, 'Once I have the baby full-time to myself, everything will be easier.' And then it would hit me; that day was not coming. This 'work' thing was not going away. There was no prolonged stretch of time in sight when it would just be the baby and me. And then I sobbed in my office for ten minutes. The same ten minutes that magazines urge me to use for sit-ups and triceps dips, I used for sobbing. Of course I'm not supposed to admit that there is a triannual torrential sobbing in my office, because it's bad for the feminist cause. It makes it harder for women to be taken seriously in the workplace. But I have friends who stay home with their kids and they also have a triannual sob, so I think we should call it even."

Here's the good news for me: Tina Fey is approximately one zillion times busier than I am. If she can make it work with only a triannual sob, then my potential future seems considerably less daunting. Plus, I *love* a good sob. Why else would I keep watching *Grey's Anatomy*?

As my nose-to-the-grindstone, eat-sleep-work month continues, the hardest part is incorporating these goals with all the changes I've adopted already. I've said it before, and I'll say it again: Time is the issue. There are only so many hours in the day, and the time spent channeling Jennifer on the treadmill or Gwyneth in the kitchen or Sarah Jessica in the closet are taking away from the time I'd like to spend, or rather, feel like I *should* spend, typing away, Tina-style.

It's that pesky perfectionism thing creeping in again. The more I read *InStyle* or *People* and see photos of stars being just like me, the more I think I should be able to do it all. The celebrities splashed across *Us Weekly* always seem to be perfectly dressed and perfectly toned while shopping for the ingredients to bake a homemade birthday cake, or they look impeccable while reading a script, pregnant and adorable, while at brunch with their perfect husbands. Rarely does someone admit that, "Hey, it takes hours to get this body, and between the exercise and work I have no time to cook. I'm all about microwave meals!" Every now and then a celebrity will mention, briefly and in passing, that she enlists help, but it's always mentioned as an afterthought. Like Sarah Jessica Parker in an interview with Oprah, where she casually and indirectly mentions her housekeeper: "[When I try on clothes to go out], I leave a mess and then I feel crappy about it. Before I left home today, I left a note saying, 'I apologize for the state of the closet. Don't touch a thing in there! I'll clean it all up when I get back.'" Do these A-listers so rarely mention their help because they don't want to seem out of touch with the everywoman? Or do they really want their fans to believe they're regular people, with superhuman powers when it comes to doing it all? The latter message seems much more detrimental. It's healthier for regular folks to hear that, sure, you *can* have it all when you can afford to hire a staff, rather than that Angelina raises six kids, travels the globe, maintains a killer figure, volunteers around the world, and continues to work . . . and *you should, too.*

You can imagine my relief, then, to learn that Tina Fey does not work out. That's right. Not at all. According to Tina, she doesn't have time to spend an hour a day at the gym. "Even yoga classes go on 80 or 90 minutes," she told *Harper's Bazaar.* "You will still die. I'll do grave yoga. Someone can come and stretch me in my grave." Instead, Tina admits to losing thirty pounds on Weight Watchers before going on camera for *Saturday Night Live.* "I try to delude myself that I'm in the old-Hollywood mode. I just tailor my clothes and try to keep my skin clear."

Of course, my type-A tendencies haven't allowed me to use this as an excuse to stop exercising altogether—Jennifer's body is nowhere in reach if I'm not exercising five days a week—but it does provide some insight into the fact that maybe these superstars aren't actually all doing it all.

———

In their book *Good Enough Is the New Perfect,* authors Becky Gillespie and Hollee Temple address the extreme perfectionism that they say is pervasive among mothers today. After extensive research, they found that one of the main reasons mothers are so hard on themselves is that they are constantly comparing themselves to the moms around them. "We see her everywhere, that specter of maternal perfection," Gillespie and Temple write. "She's at Gymboree, asking sweetly, 'How much sign language does Carter know? Landon can sign apple, kale, and toilet—and he's only nine months old!' And at the playground, smiling serenely as she passes a slice of organic pumpkin millet loaf to her toddler while we dig through our own bags, praying for a stray granola bar or a bag of chips to satiate our own child. We see her at school, shepherding her tightly braided and well-matched kindergartner into the classroom while she signs up to run the Halloween party *and* the book fair. (We're sure she never forgets to turn in field-trip money or send sneakers on gym day.) And she's at work, exuding the healthy glow of a woman who has never arrived in the office with Cheerios in her hair and someone's empty juice box in her handbag. It doesn't matter that this woman exists only as a composite. In our minds, she's there, and she's succeeding where we fail."

The reality, Gillespie and Temple explain, is that the mom who bakes organic millet loaf might send her daughter out in mismatched socks, and the office mom with the Cheerio-less hair probably hasn't had time to teach her one-year-old sign language. The woman who is "perfect" in one area is probably less so in another, and it's only in our heads that the mom with the perfectly groomed child and the one who serves only homemade organic food and the one who runs the school bake sale and the one who excels in the office are all one and the same.

As it turns out, I've been creating my own composite of perfection. Where the subjects in *Good Enough Is the New Perfect* are using other mothers to comprise their golden standard, I am using celebrities. We non-moms are not immune to the dangers of comparison and self-judgment, we just use different models. We learn that Jennifer Aniston works out nearly two hours a day, Gwyneth cooks all her own gourmet meals, Sarah Jessica always looks adorable, Tina is constantly working, Jennifer Garner keeps up a loving marriage, and Julia Roberts meditates . . . and we magically composite all those traits into one untouchable superhuman that we should emulate. Clearly that's what I've done, and I know I'm not alone. Other people's composite celebrity might be different—Amy Poehler's sense of humor combined with Jennifer Lawrence's body paired with Gwen Stefani's family life, plus, say, Kate Middleton's poise and Halle Berry's style—but the pressure is the same. When I posted a poll on Facebook asking people which celebrity lifestyle they'd most want for themselves, not one person wrote: "The pressure of the celebrity existence seems too stressful. When the cameras stop rolling, I bet they're unhappy . . . I'd rather be me!" Instead comments read like wish lists: "I want to be funny and sweet like Mindy Kaling." "I would like the whole life of Gwyneth Paltrow. I secretly have dreams that I'm friends with her, and that my husband and I double date with her and Chris." "Gwen Stefani's overall package—fitness, love, family and talent!" Or my personal favorite, "Kate Middleton's husband—does that count?"

The most popular response to my informal survey wasn't that people want the lifestyle of any single celebrity; they want a combination of many. Creating aspirational superstar composites is almost irresistible. Remembering that we've created these models of perfection in our heads—that they exist only in our mind, and not in reality—is the hard part.

The simple reality that Tina Fey doesn't work out, or at least claims not to, pulls the myth of the composite celebrity into focus. Jennifer Aniston probably doesn't always cook her own meals. Jennifer Garner may not have time for meditation. If I had to bet, I'd guess Tina doesn't cook at home that often, either. They each make choices and prioritize. And if they can't, or don't, do it all—even with all the trappings and privileges that come along with celebrity—why should I?

If I want to be as creatively productive as Tina Fey, some other commitments will have to give.

Of course, knowing something intellectually and actually incorporating that knowledge into my daily life are two different things. So despite this Tina Fey–inspired epiphany, I still find myself trying to do it all. (And I've still got four more celebs to go. Yikes.) But, thanks to Tina, I'm less hard on myself when I fall short.

The perfect day, so far, looks something like this: Wake up and head straight to the gym. Spend an hour working out—high intensity interval training that alternates between treadmill runs and strength training. Go home, shower, pick out an adorable outfit that makes me look and feel stylish and confident. Grab my computer bag and head to the coffee shop where I spend the day hunkered over the computer. Make a quick run to the grocery store for dinner ingredients. Cook said dinner. Return to the computer for more work. Email. Blog. Unwind in front of the TV while simultaneously doing Gwyneth's arm workout or Jennifer's yoga or pilates. Sleep.

On paper, this day sounds not especially difficult or unusual or even accomplished. I'm almost embarrassed that a) I only rarely knock off every one of those tasks (the nightly cooking, after-dinner work, and nighttime exercise don't always make the cut) and b) it has taken me a carefully plotted celebrity-driven quest to get this far.

But it's not as if before this challenge I didn't ever exercise, get dressed, go to work, or cook (if only occasionally). The goal of living a bit more like the stars of *Us Weekly* didn't suddenly pull me out of a reclusive existence that subsisted solely on bed rest and *New Girl*. What these last few months have changed is the attitude with which I approach these areas of my life. There is enthusiasm, drive, and purpose where there was once merely resignation. Associating a goal, or even just a role model, with each bit of my life—even something as small as getting dressed—has given me something to work toward. Even small goals provide intention.

Not to sound all Oprah, but acting with intention, even if that intention is to look more like a celebrity, really does make life more enjoyable.

And the satisfaction of *having done* what I set out to do? Even if that's just writing down some words or throwing together an adorable outfit? That feels pretty great.

As for the fact that I only check off all the items on my to-do list on rare days, and that it's usually the late-in-the-day tasks that I skimp on, I'm pleased to report this isn't evidence of my laziness. It's science. Oh, how I love when I can chalk my failures up to a force larger than myself.

Turns out I've got a simple case of ego depletion.

Ego depletion is the idea that we only have so much willpower to draw from, so it's harder to stick to our resolve later in the day, once we've already made a number of good decisions. In his 2012 *New York Times* article "Be It Resolved," journalist John Tierney writes about this phenomenon with regard to New Year's resolutions. "Most people are not going to keep their resolutions all year long. They'll start out with the best of intentions but the worst of strategies, expecting that they'll somehow find the willpower to resist temptation after temptation. By the end of January, a third will have broken their resolutions, and by July more than half will have lapsed. They'll fail because they'll eventually run out of willpower, which social scientists no longer regard as simply a metaphor. They've recently reported that willpower is a real form of mental energy, powered by glucose in the bloodstream, which is used up as you exert self-control."

While Tierney's article deals with ego depletion over the course of a year, the concept is at play from day to day as well. If a person spends all her mental energy on not indulging in pancakes at brunch and forcing herself to go to the gym, it will be harder for her to pass on that cookie, or cigarette, or insert-your-vice-of-choice, later.

The solution then, it seems to me, would be to knock out all your healthy resolutions at the beginning of the day. That's not always possible, of course. I'm not going to cook dinner at 9 A.M., though maybe I should do that second pilates or yoga workout right when I get home from my first hour of exercise. Tierney's prescription might be more realistic: To be more successful, he says, people should use their willpower less, not more. As in, don't force yourself to resist M&Ms, just don't keep M&Ms in your house. Control your environment. "Instead of fending off one urge after another," he writes, "[successful resolvers] set up their lives to minimize temptations. They play offense, not defense, using their willpower in advance so that they avoid crises, conserve their energy and outsource as much self-control as they can."

The good news is that most of my resolutions are proactive, rather than focused on the negative, which should make success easier. "Work out twice a day, four days a week" or "cook more" aren't about resisting temptation the way "eat less" or "stop smoking" might be. But of course all my new goals have a flip side. "Get to the gym" could be reinterpreted as "resist the snooze button." "Do at-home exercises whenever I watch TV" is another way of saying "ignore the lure of the couch at night." Since it's my nighttime resolutions that are taking the biggest hit, perhaps there are small changes I could make to implement Tierney's advice. If I watch TV in my bedroom, rather than the living room, maybe I'll be keener to do some Tracy Anderson arms as I watch *Parenthood,* since there's no couch in there. I wouldn't feel tempted to get into bed at that point, because it would feel too early.

I thought the appeal of looking like Jennifer Aniston would be motivation enough to follow all my new resolutions, but I'm human. It's easy to slip every now and then. Tricking my brain in order to make success easier couldn't hurt.

* * *

A week or so after Matt's appointment with the urologist, I get my doctor on the phone. After relaying the urologist's suggestions, I explain to him my confusion. "If we're going to end up doing IVF anyway, I don't understand what the extra couple of months will do."

"To be honest, I don't either," he says. "Given your test results, I don't think any lifestyle changes are going to fix the problem." It's too bad, since lifestyle changes have been my specialty over the last few months. If only modeling myself after the superfertile Jessica Simpson or Tori Spelling could improve this aspect of my life. I'd trade a Gwyneth-style kitchen or an SJP wardrobe for a celebrity-style pregnancy any day. "A lot of people like to try everything before they do IVF, but if your urologist says it won't work it's probably not worth trying."

"That's how I feel," I say. "I just want to make something happen."

"If your end goal is to get pregnant, then you should go ahead and pursue the IVF," he says.

If my end goal is to get pregnant?

The conversation ends with my doctor's promise to send me recommendations of reproductive endocrinologists and IVF clinics by the end of the day.

So it seems decided. Matt and I will likely go the in vitro fertilization route. I'm feeling simultaneously nervous and invigorated.

Of course, making an appointment with a fertility specialist doesn't mean we have to move ahead with this plan of action. We're exploring our options. But if this month of Tina Fey has been about working hard, it might also be about knowing when your work is done. As Tina once wrote in *The New Yorker:* "You have to try your hardest to be at the top of your game and improve every joke until the last possible second, but then you have to let it go. You can't be that kid at the top of the waterslide, overthinking it. You have to go down the chute. You have to let people see what you wrote. It will never be perfect, but perfect is overrated."

The waterslide analogy applies to my pregnancy pursuit, too. Matt and I have tried, and we could keep trying, doing what we can to improve our chances, hoping to finally hit the jackpot. But when the professionals are saying your work is probably done, you might as well listen and let go.

What I want is a baby. How I get there, at this point, is less important. I'm willing to let go, to give myself over to the medical prowess of a reproductive endocrinologist.

And if all goes as planned, one of these days I might even be able to relate to a different Tina Fey analogy: "[Childbirth] is a torturous experience with an eventual release and possible pride. In that way, sure, writing is just like having a kid."

* * *

A month spent focused on work is a lot less glamorous than time spent on fabulous clothes or absurd cleanses. To her credit, Tina Fey doesn't do much, at least publicly, that would fall in the category of out-of-touch celebrity. (I just received a Goop newsletter that included a recipe for "crispy romanesco with lemon aioli," and the picture had all of nine little broccoli florets on a plate. Is that supposed to be a meal?) "My daily life consists of going to work or being at home," she told the *Daily Mail*. So while it's been less exciting, and certainly less fun, than my previous tasks (well, maybe working out twice a day wasn't so exciting—but the looser pants were) it has certainly been productive. And enlightening. I've made some discoveries about my work habits. For example, I've learned that I write at a pace of about 500 words an hour. Faster if I'm really on a roll, but taking into consideration my massive procrastination techniques that even a little Fey-worship can't shake (thanks, Facebook), 500 per hour is a good bet. I try to write 1,000 words during any given session, so two hours is my ideal chunk of uninterrupted writing time, but if I can crank out about two pages—or 500 words—in any free hour-long period, they add up. Good to know.

I've also learned that there's no ideal location for my work.

I've tried repeatedly to figure out a specific work routine that consists of getting to the same place at the same time and doing the same work for the same hours, but it just isn't taking. Some days I can be productive at home, other days I need to go to the coffee shop. Still other days I like the library, or my local diner, or even my mother's apartment when she's not home. There's something nice about being alone in a place where I can raid the fridge or do jumping jacks for an energy boost, but there's no laundry or messy bedroom to distract me.

As I read more about Tina's work habits, I have to accept that there are some things I just can't make work. No matter how much it might make me feel like the real thing, I am simply unable to write through the midnight hours. Maybe this is a sign I'm growing up, because until a year ago, late-night was my prime writing time. I often had Friday nights where I would go out, lay off the alcohol, and then come home around midnight and work until three. Not anymore.

On the days where I feel like a failure because I didn't write for all the hours I resolved to, I have to ask myself: Why am I *trying* to work until 1 A.M.? If I had to guess, I'd bet that Tina would be thrilled to sleep during those nights when she's working all hours instead. If she had the time to get her work done during the day, and didn't have to balance it with raising two kids, maybe she'd opt for working from 10–7 and calling it a day. In the quest to be more like my celebrity role models, to achieve a life more like their seemingly fabulous ones, I forget, sometimes, to ask myself the obvious question: Would this action improve my life and make me happier?

Will exercising more make me happier? Yes.

Will trading microwave meals for home-cooked ones improve my mood? Yes.

Will attending to my career in a more focused and productive way make me feel better about myself? Yes.

Will working through the night instead of sleeping bring me joy? No.

Could it be that sometimes, every now and then, like on the days I'm exhausted and would love nothing more than a whopping nine hours of sleep, that being me is actually *better* than being Tina? It's hard to believe, but maybe so.

With our obsessive celebrity culture comes the notion that whatever our favorite stars do, we should do, too. Just look at the cover lines on any women's magazine: "Get a Belly Like Bilson!" (*Women's Health*) "Gwyneth's Slim-Body Secrets!" (*Self*) "Lessons From the World's Sexiest Women!" (*Allure*) The message is clear: Follow their lead, and you will be a better, more fabulous person. For those more blinded by stardom than even I, that idea can lead to bad decisions. Think botched plastic surgery and prolonged stays in rehab. I like to think I'm more levelheaded, that I know the difference between a celebrity role model and a celebrity train wreck. But once I've deemed someone the former, I have to remember to evaluate her actions for their potential effect on me before following them blindly. After all, Tina Fey never once said, "Here's my advice: Work through the night! Give up sleep! This is the secret to career success and happiness." Rather she explained that her at-home all-nighter, surrounded by colleagues, was the "best worst thing ever."

If I had a slew of projects in the works and a staff of comedians to surround myself with, the whole "work, work, only work" thing might be fun in a totally demented, let's-get-drunk-on-sleep-deprivation sort of way. A college friend and I were recently reminiscing about the time, sophomore year, when we had two papers due the next day for our Jewish-German Literature class. Neither of us had started, so we pulled an all-nighter and made it through by drinking too many cans of Coke and making up songs about our professor. It is, to this day, the only thing either of us remember about the course. Granted I was nineteen then, but I could see that being the best worst thing ever, even today. But working in a quiet office by myself until 3 A.M. just doesn't cut it. And I think Tina would agree.

Another lesson: One can only juggle a million things like Tina Fey if one has a million things to juggle. There's a saying "If you want something done, ask a busy person." I've always found that to be true. I have an easier time being productive when I have twenty things on my to-do list than when I have two. I thrive on the rush of chasing deadlines. And yet I usually try to give my work a singular focus. I'll aim to take on one project at a time, because I've read that multitasking makes people less efficient. Researching Tina's varied career has reminded me that it's okay to force my brain to shift gears, and add a little bit of the "How will I get it all done?" pressure. There's a fine line between having enough on your plate and too much, but I've been using this month to pitch some more projects. The handful of extra assignments I've received have provided the necessary pick-me-up. In the moments when I can't stand to write anymore, there's research to be done. When I want a more mindless activity, I can transcribe an interview and still feel productive. Having more work, it turns out, provides the freedom to do different types of work. For me, it has the opposite effect than one would expect: More work actually decreases my sense of burnout.

* * *

Obviously, work ethic isn't something captured in a photograph. You can't look at a celebrity's "Stars—They're Just Like Us!" close-up and know if she's a workaholic. But you can sense her confidence, a by-product of a job well done. The best thing about Tina is that she oozes confidence. She doesn't apologize for her success. She's earned it, and she knows it.

The further along I get on this quest, the more sure I am that the supposed perfection I'm striving for is more a matter of perception than reality. I imagine almost nobody actually feels perfect, not even Jennifer or Gwyneth, but if you feel satisfied in the moment and confident in yourself, you'll show it. If you feel like you've got your life under control, you'll look the part. And I'm learning it's the little things—a pair of cute shoes or a met deadline, rather than a $5 million mansion or private jet—that make the difference.

I have eight celebrities on my Ideal Celebrity Lifestyle list, which means I should be halfway done with this journey. On the quest for a more perfect existence, do I feel halfway there? Probably not. I wouldn't feel ready to be shot for the pages of *People,* if I were in fact a celebrity. But I most definitely feel like a better version of myself, which is something. A big something. I still may not have it all together, but I have some of it together.

People have asked me if I really needed the celebrity influence to make the changes I have thus far. You don't need Jennifer Aniston to tell you it's important to exercise, they say. Everyone knows you'll have a better outlook when you put on clothes that make you feel good about yourself rather than wearing yoga pants all day.

This is true. For the über–self-aware, it might be easy to say, "I seem to be in a funk. What areas of my life would make me feel like I have a better handle on things? What could I do to gain control and confidence? How can I make myself feel fabulous?" And maybe that person, so much more in touch with herself than I, would pinpoint that it's her lack of exercise and too many microwave meals and a dwindling enthusiasm for work that has her down. But that isn't me.

When you feel like the lifestyle you want has gotten away from you, a complete overhaul is overwhelming. You don't always know where to start. Comparing yourself to others isn't necessarily the healthiest method of self-improvement, but if it's an impetus to at least get started, is that so wrong? At the start of this pursuit, every time I flipped through another magazine, or saw another celebrity's picture online, it hit me that "I wish I had her this," or "If only I had her that." I'm not delusional. I know that no matter how many changes I make to my life, I'll never become, say, Beyoncé. But those moments of wishing provided a starting point. My thought process went from "I feel blah and so I might as well lie on the couch" to "Maybe if I did this one thing, I'd get even the tiniest jolt of her pep."

So while it may be obvious that improving your fitness and your appearance and reigniting your enthusiasm for your career would be stepping stones to a more fabulous life, it can be healthy to have reminders. It's easy for people to hate on our celebrity culture, but when approached in a healthy way, like author Jake Halpern said, there's nothing wrong with having role models.

And if you'd rather tell everyone that Marie Curie or Michelle Obama or Hillary Clinton is your hero, and only worship Tina or Gwyneth or Beyoncé in the privacy of your own guilty-pleasure tabloid binges, so be it. Your secret's safe with me.

CHAPTER FIVE

JENNIFER GARNER'S MARRIAGE

"The rule with marriage is that the less you talk about it the better." —The Independent

"One thing that makes it not not work is that we're both pretty nice. He's not someone who's ever going to blow up on anyone. What I mean is, if he's ever angry with me, he doesn't act out on it in a weird way and yell at me. And I am the same. So we can handle conflict in a very loving and adult way." —Marie Claire

"I can live with Ben working crazy hours. But I can't live without girlfriends around to talk about men with! It's fine if he's not there; I just need someone to bitch about it to!" —W Magazine

It's a tricky thing, picking a celebrity relationship to admire, and even emulate. We never know what goes on behind closed doors. The public front and the real relationship could be, and likely are, completely different. And then there's the sad reality that every couple of months another divorce makes headlines, and sometimes that divorce involves the very couple you thought had it all. A few years ago, I would have pegged Heidi Klum and Seal as *the* celebrity couple. I'd seen them on *Oprah,* talking about how lucky and in love they were. They had renewed their vows every year since their 2005 wedding, they explained. Granted the episode in question aired in 2007, so those renewals happened all of twice at that point, but theirs seemed a fairy-tale marriage.

Until they got divorced.

In Hollywood, you can never be sure of who will break up next.

A handful of celebrity relationships have stood the test of time. Tom Hanks and Rita Wilson, Goldie Hawn and Kurt Russell, Will Smith and Jada Pinkett Smith, and Warren Beatty and Annette Bening, to name a few, have all made it for about two decades or more. Not exactly the sixty-plus years that my grandparents made it work, or even the thirty of my own parents, but still mighty long in Hollywood years. And while I've gleaned plenty of marriage advice from my parents, grandparents, and in-laws—all of them stayed together till death did them part—there is something especially glamorous about Hollywood romances. It's largely the media's doing, tracking a couple's courtship and creating a story that takes fans from the very first public display of affection, or even a secret date, all the way to the walk down the aisle. We can watch our favorite couples stroll the red carpet together, vacation in the Maldives, or have dinner at Spago. I can't say that I envy the constant monitoring—the never-ending scrutiny most certainly adds pressure that my marriage will never know—but as a consumer of all this media attention, I can't help but get swept up in the fairy tale of it all.

The fascination with celebrity couples is nothing new. While our interest in watching starlets take out the trash or shop for groceries is a modern phenomenon, Americans have been captivated by off-screen romances for decades. Actors Douglas Fairbanks and Mary Pickford, who married in 1920, are considered the first superstar duo. Their romance fascinated not just the nation but the world. And before there was Brangelina or TomKat or Kimyé, there was Humphrey Bogart and Lauren Bacall, Spencer Tracy and Katharine Hepburn, and Elizabeth Taylor and Richard Burton.

Some celebrity couples seem to relish the spotlight. They sign up for reality TV shows or do interviews with Barbara Walters, reminding the world of their combined star power. But other duos of A-listers, when captured by the camera, appear totally romantic but also exceedingly down-to-earth. They try to keep their names out of headlines, which only makes us love them more (they want to be normal! they want to make it!), and in those rare moments when we do see them together, we swoon.

Jennifer Garner and Ben Affleck are the embodiment of that seemingly normal celebrity marriage. Since their 2005 wedding, they've been one of Hollywood's most adored pairs. They rarely make joint public appearances (though they were a fan-favorite fixture of the 2013 *Argo*-heavy awards season), so when they appear in the tabloids, it's usually a paparazzi shot with their three kids at the park, or cheering for the Red Sox at Fenway. They seem like any regular couple, except infinitely more beautiful and rich and famous. They're the all-American celebrity pairing—exactly how we picture ourselves if we were famous and married and could have anyone we wanted.

Of course, Ben Affleck knew what it was to be in a high-profile celebrity romance before he married his wife. He was at the center of a media firestorm from 2002 to 2004, when he dated another Jennifer. He and Jennifer Lopez were "Bennifer," the original combined celebrity nickname. Week after week, for a year and a half, they made the cover of every tabloid on the newsstand. Ben appeared in J.Lo's music video "Jenny from the Block" wearing a white robe and giving the singer's backside a baby oil rubdown.

They did a joint *Dateline* interview that attracted 10.6 million viewers. They co-starred in *Gigli,* widely considered one of Hollywood's worst films. I don't need to tell you how this all worked out. The media had a field day with the couple's eighteen-month romance, and an even bigger one with their breakup. It hurt Affleck's public image, and his career. As Ben's friend Matt Damon told *The Hollywood Reporter:* "I remember Ben calling and saying: 'I can sell magazines and not movies. I'm in the worst possible place I can be.'"

Shortly after the first Bennifer ended, another one began. Ben Affleck and Jennifer Garner started dating in 2004, making their inaugural public appearance together at the first Red Sox World Series game. They got married in 2005, had a baby that same year, and have done their best to keep a low profile ever since. They haven't appeared in a movie together since *Daredevil,* which came out around the time their romance began, and Jennifer has said many times that she doesn't plan on working with her husband again any time soon. "He's brilliant at what he does, but why rock the boat?" she asked *W* magazine in 2010. "It works between us pretty well the way it is. I don't know if I want to go to work with him. I'd be like, 'Okay already, you got the shot. Let's go home!'"

They don't do interviews together. They have largely handled their relationship in the exact opposite fashion of the first Bennifer, and it has certainly worked to their advantage.

In a Biography channel special all about Ben and Jen, celebrity and entertainment reporters repeatedly describe the couple as "normal," "down-to-earth," and "regular." Having both already been one half of a failed celebrity romance (Jen was married to actor Scott Foley for nearly three years), it appears that they were determined to lay low the second time around. Instead of walking the red carpet, they took family trips to the playground. Jennifer, with her West Virginia upbringing, girl-next-door dimples, and dedication to motherhood, seemed like any new parent you might meet at Mommy and Me. Ben reshaped his image into down-to-earth family man. As one commentator on the Biography special explained, "They are seen as hands-on parents, and they seem genuinely happy to be parents." That they do this while still maintaining careers and appearing on covers of *Esquire* or *InStyle* is why we'll never forget that while they might *seem* regular, they aren't. We're reminded that they're famous and in love when, at the Golden Globes, best director Ben tells the world that Jennifer is his "everything."

I'm not the only one who thinks Ben and Jen have what it takes to make it for the long haul. Even *The New York Times* has named Jennifer Garner and Ben Affleck one of the most likely celebrity couples to survive. In the 2006 article "From Tinseltown to Splitsville: Just Do the Math," journalist John Tierney (the same one who taught me about ego-depletion and willpower) teamed up with Garth Sundem, author of *Geek Logik*, to formulate the Sundem/Tierney Unified Celebrity Theory, "an equation for predicting the odds that a celebrity marriage will last." The formula takes into consideration the couple's combined number of previous marriages (Jen and Ben: one, Jennifer's to Foley), their ages, their level of fame (first determined by the number of hits when googling their names, recently revised to the ratio of mentions in the *Times* divided by mentions in the *National Enquirer*), how long they knew each other before getting married, and her sex symbol status (specifically: "Of her first five Google hits, the number showing her in clothing [or lack thereof] designed to elicit libidinous thoughts"). The Sundem/Tierney Unified Celebrity Theory correctly predicted the breakups of Tom and Katie, Ashton and Demi, Pamela Anderson and Kid Rock, and Britney Spears and Kevin Federline. According to the formula, Ben and Jen had a roughly even chance of lasting five years. They've currently been married nearly a decade.

Of course, Ben and Jen could break up tomorrow. I'd be surprised—the entire celeb-obsessed world would be shocked—but this is Hollywood. It could happen.

I have a pretty great marriage. Matt and I rarely fight. We love spending time together, but still encourage each other to be independent. We support each other's decisions, make each other laugh, and finish each other's sentences. We sleep with one body part touching, even if it's our toes. I don't feel like my relationship is a chaotic mess, which is the way I felt about my exercise and work regimen, my cooking and eating, and my wardrobe. Those things all needed overhauls when this year started, while my marriage is in a good place. But there's always room for improvement, and thus far this journey has been fairly self-centered. It might be nice to turn my attention outward. It's easy to get so caught up in personal self-improvement that you forget about the people around you, and a stellar marriage is vital to an overall happy life, which is the ultimate goal of this celebrity pursuit. Plus, given our whole baby chase and the stress it can put on a relationship, now is probably a good time to give Matt a little extra loving.

In the scheme of infertility issues, Matt and I are lucky. We pinpointed the problem relatively early, so hopefully we won't suffer through years of struggle. The doctors we've spoken to sound confident that I'll get pregnant, somehow. Plenty of people have had a rougher go of it than I, so I'm grateful we've been proactive and have already started on a course to getting a baby. That said, I'm still nursing a deep-seated sadness at not having a little one on the way, and it's not always easy to maintain perspec-tive. The moments of tension at home these days root from my frustration with not being pregnant, and Matt's frustration with my frustration. He thinks I'm being melodramatic for someone who's only been trying for ten months, and I wish he'd be more understanding when he finds me crying because another friend just called to say she's expecting.

We have our first appointment with the reproductive endocri-nologist next week, and I know Matt's feeling conflicted. He wants to get the show on the road—while he may not be as des-perate for a baby as I am, I know he's disappointed that I'm not pregnant—but he doesn't want to jump the gun or make a big decision too hastily. He considers it his job to be the cautious, thoughtful one in response to my impatience. But even before we meet the doctor, the one thing I know is that infertility can put a strain on a marriage. It can put undue pressure on a couple, screw up a sex life, and cause resentment. I don't think that will be Matt and me—we've withstood a lot over the ten years we've been together—but it couldn't hurt to give my marriage some extra attention.

* * *

Like any pop-culture-devouring fan, I clearly have strong feelings about the stars I've met only in the pages of magazines. While Jen and Ben are adorable, and I really liked *13 Going on 30*, I've never had much to say about Jennifer Garner. I have a bit of a BFF-complex with Tina Fey and idol worship for Jennifer Aniston, but Jennifer Garner has always been, just, fine.

Not anymore.

Profiles of the actress paint her as the kindest, most down-to-earth, lovable starlet in all of Hollywood. She puts her family first. She wears accessible clothes when she's out with her kids. One article tells how she declined an offer to be upgraded to first class when the airline messed up her reservation. (Can you imagine getting settled in coach and finding Jennifer Garner in the middle seat?) "Garner gardens, waxes rhapsodic about the recipes in *The Foster's Market Cookbook* ('chicken, spaghetti squash, roasted tomatoes'), enjoys cleaning closets—'my former roommate will tell you that I was the person to scrub the bathroom'—and says a good date night with Affleck is if she's at the stove and there's Scrabble involved," writes journalist Alexandra Jacobs in a 2006 *Elle* profile of the star. All the articles read the same: She's gracious without being apologetic for her good fortune, she's focused first on being a mother and is willing to work less so that she can be around while Ben's on the job, and she's obsessed with Martha Stewart.

When I asked a friend, one who has strong opinions about most celebrities (hates: Jennifer Aniston, Jennifer Hudson; loves: Beyoncé, Kristen Bell), how she felt about Garner, she summed it up perfectly: "I like her. I like that she doesn't seem to be too caught up in the Hollywood game. I think she's relatable and I kind of like that she doesn't seem to have lost all her baby weight already. She seems normal."

In all my research about Jennifer Garner, the thing I'm most struck by (and I do appreciate her seemingly rational attitude regarding baby weight) is just how kindly she talks about her husband. Any wife should have nice things to say about her partner, especially if she is an A-lister talking to the likes of *InStyle* or *Marie Claire*. But it's almost beyond kindness. Jennifer gushes about Ben with such reverence, such deep respect and admiration, that it's actually kind of touching. Take this nugget, from *Marie Claire* in 2007: "When he's listening to someone—and this can be someone he meets in the street, his brother, anyone whom he's standing next to in line—if he clicks into them, he can stand in one spot for hours. It's amazing." Or this, from *InStyle* in 2012: "Honestly, I would do anything for that man, because I know it's not taken for granted." In a quick scan of the interviews I've read, she describes her husband as "sexy," "kind," "understanding," "compassionate," "generous," "sweet," "nice," "impressive," "disciplined," "brilliant," and "gentlemanly." This fact in itself—*Jen has nice things to say about the man she married!*—isn't especially newsworthy, but it does make me think about my own relationship. I love Matt, a lot, and anyone who knows me knows that. But because of that love, I find it easy to make a quick joke at his expense when I'm with a group of people. Little cracks here and there are always good for a laugh, and since I consider them harmless nothings, and people know I adore my husband, no one has to feel awkward or guilty or wonder if there's some backhanded insult at play. But still, reading these interviews, it strikes me that Jennifer Garner never once pokes fun or makes a jab at Ben. The closest she comes is in an interview with Ellen DeGeneres, when she announces that Ben "kind of excels at playing Baby Doll" and that he has "wonder sperm," both of which get a laugh from the audience but are, in fact, compliments.

In interviews about his wife and family, Ben is the same way. He admits his luck at finding a great wife, and expresses gratitude for what a wonderful hands-on mother she is. In an interview with *The Hollywood Reporter,* he explains: "Jennifer played such a profound role in making me a better person. We don't have a perfect marriage, but she inspired me. . . . She truly is kind. She means no one any harm. She doesn't have ill will for any person. She's not competitive with other people. She's not spiteful. It's one of those things where it becomes almost aggravating at times. Every time I go, 'F—him!' I see in her face that she just thinks that's petty and small."

It's almost enough to make me hate them—their perfect marriage and perfect love and perfect kids, blah blah blah—if they weren't both so likable.

I don't, and never will, know what Jennifer Garner says about her husband when she's among family or friends. She probably gets annoyed at him occasionally or complains when warranted or playfully teases him at the dinner table. But the united front they present, and their obvious respect for each other, is admirable. And so, to make my marriage more like the Garner-Afflecks', my first resolution is simple: Speak only kindly of Matt in public. Always show to others how much I respect him. No silly jokes, no frustrated eye rolls. Notable exceptions: Complaints can be made to my very best friends. A girl's got to vent sometimes.

The Garner plan, part one, is embarrassingly simple: Honor thy husband.

* * *

Today is Sunday, which means it's the perfect day to enact part two of my relationship-boosting plan. Matt is where he often is on Sunday afternoons: the couch, watching football. Even when his beloved Patriots aren't playing, Matt can be heard screaming at the TV from down the hall. During this time, I could be any number of places: at yoga class, shopping with a friend, on the phone, or in our bedroom watching *Two Weeks Notice*. Anywhere but with him.

I know plenty of female football fans. I've always wanted to be one of them—women who can talk with me about *Downton Abbey* and just as easily to Matt about Tom Brady have always struck me as much cooler than I. I've never had much interest in watching sports, other than the NCAA tournament, and that's only because I love to fill out brackets and enter pools. (I may not love sports, but I love gambling.) Sometimes I mistake myself for a sports fan because I was an athlete in high school and for a moment I'll think the two are related. If Matt has friends over to watch the game, I may even plant myself on the couch and try to be one of the guys. If I had something to add to the "greatest of all time" debates—Chamberlain vs. Russell, Brady vs. Manning, Jordan vs. Lebron—maybe I'd earn a spot at the table. Instead, after about five minutes, I'll inevitably pull out a *People* to flip through while the arguments rage around me.

If there's one thing that Ben Affleck and my husband have in common, besides their handsome good looks, it's their Boston roots. Both are die-hard Red Sox, Patriots, and Celtics fans. When Ben and Jennifer Garner got together, she got on board with Boston. They went to Red Sox and Celtics games, and Jennifer even proved her stuff on a 2009 episode of *The Jay Leno Show* when she was challenged to name the entire Red Sox starting lineup. She'd never been a baseball fan before, she told the press, but since it was on all the time in her house, she grew to like it. "I think that [games] are like soap operas," she told *Marie Claire*. "If you watch five in a row, you know enough to get hooked."

I could never be a true Red Sox fan. I grew up in a New York Mets household—my dad had season tickets—so I won't give up my allegiance to that team, even if they haven't put up much of a showing in recent years. Football, though, was never a big deal in my childhood home. My father and brother watched games together, but they never had a strong passion for anyone in particular. Thus, my allegiance is up for grabs, and I'm willing to become a New England Patriots fan for the good of my marriage.

"I'm going to watch football with you now," I declare as I wander into our living room.

"Really?" Matt looks surprised, but intrigued.

"Yes. Jennifer Garner watches with Ben Affleck," I tell him. "It's going to strengthen our marriage."

Matt smirks at my reasoning, but makes room for me on the couch. Over the next couple of hours I ask a lot of questions—"Why are those guys fighting all the way over on that end when the ball is over here?" "Is that a fumble or an incomplete pass?" "How can those guys be so huge and so strong and still have that tummy hanging over their pants?"—which make Matt laugh, but he answers all of them patiently enough. Until today, my football knowledge came primarily from *Friday Night Lights* and *Remember the Titans.* But the basics—the knowledge I need to generally understand what's happening on the screen in front of me—are pretty easy to grasp. And I like asking questions. It forces some conversation into this football bonding afternoon.

It's a quiet Sunday, and Matt and I spend the next few hours watching games. The Pats aren't playing until tomorrow night, so this is like a warm-up round, and it turns out to be a pretty fantastic afternoon. The screams that usually have me rolling my eyes actually have some context, and they seem much less crazy when I'm part of the action. And what Jennifer Garner said about baseball holds true here, too—once you've watched a couple of games it's easier to get caught up in the drama. Most important, it's been a lovely afternoon for Matt and me as a couple. Psychologists say men like "side-to-side" relationships while women prefer to spend time together "face-to-face." Guys might bond over watching sports or playing golf or video games while the ladies would rather talk over a long meal. The theory explains, at least in part, why men recoil at those dreaded words "we need to talk." This whole sitting on the couch and watching football thing is very side-to-side. For Matt, it's marital bonding at its best. I like having the time together, too, and if I get an occasional cuddle out of it, even better.

Monday night is the main event. When Matt gets home from work I ask him if he has any Patriots gear I can wear. If I'm going to do this, I want to look the part. The evening consists of lots of high fives and Matt screaming, "Get it! Get in there!" and me asking Matt who he has a bigger crush on: quarterback Tom Brady or his wife, Giselle. (Answer: Too close to call.) I've also decided that if I were a football player, I'd definitely be a running back, and Matt tells me he would be a wide receiver. (Who said you can't discover new things after ten years?) The Patriots take the game handily.

The night is, in a word, fun. With to-do lists and work pressures and exhaustion after a long day, it's easy to fall into a routine at home. On most nights, Matt and I may eat dinner or watch TV together, catching up on our day or the upcoming week, but while routine can be comforting, it's not necessarily fun. I wouldn't have expected it, but cheering for the Patriots together provides a forum for us to get excited, act like kids, and be a team. Maybe it's the novelty of the activity that brings the biggest rush, but it feels like we're a couple of pals kicking back and enjoying a good time. The break from all the baby talk, and the comfort of companionship, makes us both smile.

Good old-fashioned fun is severely underrated.

I've watched three football games in two days, which is more than I usually watch in an entire season. Even in this short span, I can say that this has likely contributed more to my happiness than any other change I've made this year. It's not the football itself that is any magical marriage boost, but the one-on-one time. It's nice to be with Matt when he's doing one of the things he loves most, and while part of me worried he would find it annoying to have me yapping in his ear during the game, he seems to like the company.

A week later, Matt has friends over to watch another Patriots game. While I'm in the kitchen gathering beers, I overhear him tell a friend that "Rachel's learning about football. It's actually pretty cool."

Rock-solid evidence that investing some time into your partner's interests does not go unnoticed.

Jennifer Garner has done what nobody before her could. She turned me into a football fan.

* * *

Today is our first appointment at the fertility center. The appointment is at 7 A.M., so Matt and I are both a bit bleary-eyed when we wander into the waiting room. As we settle in, I do a quick scan of my surroundings—there are a number of couples, and some women on their own, and a few families with a young child or two. I might be the youngest in the room, and I certainly look the most lost. From the research I've done, I know that IVF and other fertility treatments often include frequent, even daily, visits to the doctor's office, and the women around me look noticeably at home here. I try to flip through a copy of *Cosmo* but am distracted by this clan of women and couples all in the same boat. I wish I could talk to them, ask them their story, or understand why it is that we all found ourselves in this situation of being unable to get the thing we want most. That some of these couples have young kids with them is at least encouraging. And if nothing else, this crowded waiting room is certainly a reminder that I'm not alone.

Matt, as usual, seems the calm and collected one to my ball of nervous energy. I want to get started, and now, but I also have a zillion questions. Matt wants to simply assess the situation, take it all in, and go from there.

Our RE, Dr. E, was highly recommended by a family friend and emailed me directly to set up the appointment. Which is to say, I already love her. She seems to be in her late thirties or early forties, with three kids of her own that she tells us were conceived through IVF. She is warm and friendly and I'm pretty sure I would ask her to be my best friend if 1) she weren't obviously too busy with being a mom and doctor who works around the clock and 2) it wasn't totally and completely inappropriate to ask my doctor on a friend date.

After some small talk, Dr. E gets down to business. "Looking at your test results, the good news is your numbers aren't that bad. I've certainly seen worse, and it's not impossible that you could get pregnant on your own." This surprises me, and makes me wonder if we should be here. "It might take ten years, but it could happen."

That's all I need to hear. I'm not on a ten-year plan. I know I'm feeling some more urgency than Matt, but I'm pretty sure even he doesn't want to wait until we're 40 to start our family. A decade of trying would be, well, trying.

Dr. E reviews our basic medical history and explains what IVF is, how it works, and how I'll feel over the next couple of months.

"I think this is going to go really well," she says. "Male factor infertility is one of the easier problems for us to deal with, and given your health and age, this should move relatively quickly."

"So, what does that mean, exactly, timewise?"

When I spoke to my OB-GYN about moving forward with IVF, he said, "You could be puking by December!" It's already October, so that seems too good to be true.

"You could be pregnant in six weeks," Dr. E says.

This is nearly impossible to believe. Six weeks! That might as well be tomorrow.

When Dr. E asks if we have any questions, Matt and I both want to know the same thing.

"Do you think it makes sense to be doing this now?" I ask her. "We're both worried that we're acting too soon, since it hasn't been a full year."

"You're doing the right thing," she says. "If your numbers were borderline and I thought you could make easy changes that would sway the results, I would tell you. But this one is pretty clear-cut."

That seems to satisfy Matt, and I'm certainly sold. The next step, Dr. E says, is to get me in for an ultrasound and for both of us to have bloodwork done. She directs us to the waiting room, and tells me that a nurse will be in touch later today to discuss my medications and other next steps.

Before we leave her office, I ask Dr. E the question I imagine she hates to hear: Considering her optimism, where would she put our chances of success?

"I'd say 60 percent," she says with smile that tells me she likes those odds.

In the waiting room, Matt and I quickly confer. We both liked Dr. E, and he's feeling reassured that we're making the right choice.

"But 60 percent," I say. "That's not even a passing grade on a test."

"But a 60 percent batting average would put us in the Hall of Fame," he counters.

This says all you need to know about the differences between Matt and me.

From the doctor's office, Matt heads to work and I go home. Any dreams of being Tina Fey–like in my productivity today are shot. I'm at peak distraction. Especially since Google is a black hole of IVF research, infertility message boards, and baby blogs. I'm consumed with questions I don't need to be asking yet. Will we transfer one egg or two? Should I stop working out right away? Do I want to tell friends that we're doing this? Will we get frozen embryos for baby number two? Will the doctor know when she does the transfer if it's a girl or a boy?

Later that same day I get a call from one nurse regarding prescriptions she's calling in for me, an email from another with an estimated time line and instructions for administering injections, and a phone call from the pharmacy confirming ten different medications. This endeavor is not to be taken lightly, and all this communication really hammers that message home. The time line is a dense document that involves endless scrolling as I read it on my iPhone. For now it only says when I should take my first birth control pill (counterintuitively, women go on the pill before starting IVF, to control the timing of the cycle) and for how long, but there are boxes to fill in dates and times for "stimulation," "trigger," "retrieval," and "transfer." I barely know what these words mean. After I finish my two weeks of birth control, I'll be going back to the office for more monitoring and bloodwork, after which I'll receive a call with my next set of directions.

The whole "sit at home and wait for the call with your instructions" thing makes me think they're going to hold my ovaries hostage, but at this point I'm resigned to whatever the doctor has planned.

I've already mentioned that this celebrity-inspired journey has been an interesting foray into the idea of control, especially since the pregnancy pursuit thus far has been so completely uncontrollable. I'm on two quests at once, and they seem completely at odds. IVF is the meeting of those minds—it's the pursuit of a baby in the most controlled environment possible. Medicines and injections and procedures are measured down to the minute, and while it lacks the spontaneity of those "it just happened!" pregnancies born of a bottle of wine and a romantic beach vacation, the reality is that Matt and I gave up on that a while ago. No matter how in love you are or how attractive your spouse, baby-making sex loses most of its excitement by about month three. There's just something about the words, "I'm ovulating, we need to do it before you go to work because we both have plans tonight," that doesn't scream romance.

It reminds me of the conversation I had with my doctor the day he called to tell me the results of Matt's semen analysis. "So you think we'll definitely get pregnant somehow, even if it's not naturally?" I asked.

"Yes," he said. "And there's nothing all that natural about baby-making sex anyway."

* * *

One thing Matt and I do well in our marriage, and I truly believe this makes for a strong relationship, is that we each make time for friends. For about two years after we moved to Chicago, I was seriously lacking local friendships. I didn't have anyone to call at the last minute for brunch on a Sunday, or to come over for a bottle of wine and a reality-TV marathon on a Friday night. I had friends to schedule dinner dates with, but even those had to be planned three weeks in advance, and over email. I wanted some-one to call "just to say hi," like the close friends I'd left behind in New York City. Even with a good job, a husband I loved, and close family nearby, my life felt noticeably incomplete without girlfriends. So I spent a year focused on making that one single change. I dedicated my personal life to the pursuit of friendship. And it worked. I met a ton of fabulous Chicago women, and de-veloped the kind of close relationships I'd been missing. In the end it had just the effect I'd hoped for. I felt more settled in Chi-cago. There was a sense of belonging and community, and Friday nights spent at home alone were no longer lonely since I knew I had plenty of pals only a phone call away.

The friendship search also changed my life in a way I hadn't anticipated: It strengthened my marriage. Not that Matt and I were having any real marital strife, but the fights we did have usu-ally stemmed from my own friendship frustration. When there was something on my mind, I longed for a close pal to hash it out with over dinner. In the absence of that friend, I looked to Matt. And while he's a fabulous husband, he's not the best girlfriend. He didn't want to analyze and overanalyze dilemmas. He wanted to offer a solution and move on to the next topic. I was usually looking for empathy rather than answers, and this difference often led to an argument. Other times, a friend from out of town would visit, and when she'd leave I'd go into a funk, feeling sorry for myself that all my closest friends were states away. This spiral of self-pity frustrated Matt, who then reminded me of all the wonderful blessings I should be grateful for, and there we'd be again, arguing.

Once I had new friends, I didn't go to Matt for my girl talk anymore. I had actual girls for that. Visits from long-distance pals made me happy, without the post-visit blues that used to plague me like a bad hangover. Matt and I had less cause for fighting, and we indeed fought much less.

To his credit, while Matt didn't necessarily relate to my sincere longing for more friends, he supported my search. He never complained that I was out of the house too much, or spending too much time with friends and not enough with him. And as I once heard him tell someone who asked how my new-friend search affected him, "Rachel was happier, and she complained less about having no friends, so I was happier."

As they say, a happy wife is a happy life.

During that year, I grew to understand the importance of male friendship, too. Not that I begrudged Matt time with his friends in the past, but I actually became something of a friendship pusher. If he planned a night at home when I went out, I'd urge (nag?) him to call the guys. "Do a boys night! It's important for your heart health!"

I've been surprised to learn that many couples our age don't have this same level of enthusiasm for girls and guys nights out. One evening, Matt and I went bowling with another couple. The game was finished around 9 P.M., so we all decided to part ways. I was going to meet some girlfriends at a bar, and Matt was going to meet a group of guys at someone's apartment. Our friend Mike was flabbergasted. "You're just going to go out, separately, and each do your own thing?" he asked, looking at Matt. "You're going to hang with buddies?" His jealousy was obvious.

Matt confirmed his suspicions.

"That is so cool," Mike said. "That's the dream."

This couple has been together two years to our ten, so maybe they'll grow into this next phase, but the exchange made me feel good about my marriage. We're both happy to go out on our own, and we always come home to the same bed at the end of the night.

I've been thinking about this aspect of marriage since reading a quote from Jennifer Garner about Ben's busy moviemaking schedule. "I can live with Ben working crazy hours," she told *W* magazine. "But I can't live without girlfriends around to talk about men with! It's fine if he's not there; I just need someone to bitch about it to!"

It's my biggest plug for maintaining friendships outside of marriage: "I can't vent to my husband about my husband." Or I can, but the result is never good.

Jen's girlfriend tidbit is a good reminder. It's amazingly easy to fall back into old habits of lying on the couch when Matt's not home rather than making a plan, and maintaining the kind of friendships where you can, as Jen says, bitch about your husband's absence, takes work. But it does so much to build satisfaction, and stave off resentment, in a marriage.

One day, when the imaginary paparazzi take a picture of my family at the park for the make-believe tabloid I've created in my head, I want us to look more Garner-Affleck than Frankel-Hoppy. I want to have that happy, engaged, and grateful smile that Jennifer sports whenever she's gazing at Ben, rather than Bethenny's scowl that made the tabloids scream, "Impending divorce!" (Which, no surprise, turned out to be true.)

It's not only Jennifer who puts a premium on friendship. Ben Affleck is perhaps as famous for his marriage as he is for his best friendship and bromance with actor, co–Oscar winner, and fellow Bostonian Matt Damon. Clearly, strong relationships are a priority with these people.

Which makes it especially fitting that Matt is out of town this weekend, on his annual Vegas trip with his best friends from high school. They've gone every year for nearly a decade, and while I'm sure they do plenty of things I don't want or need to know about and likely wouldn't approve of, I love the idea that these best friends since middle school are still going strong twenty years later.

With Matt away, I've decided to pass this solo Friday night not with friends but with the new documentary *Sellebrity*. The movie, produced and directed by entertainment photographer Kevin Mazur, looks at the commercialized world of fame, and gives first-hand insight into what it's like to get bombarded by the paparazzi from no less than Jennifer Aniston, Sarah Jessica Parker, Elton John, and Jennifer Lopez.

The picture that Mazur paints isn't a pretty one. Jennifer Lopez and Marc Anthony talk about photographers climbing over the walls of their home to get a photo. Sarah Jessica describes being chased and hiding in a nearby hotel lobby. J.Lo, Sarah Jessica, Jennifer Aniston, Salma Hayek, Sheryl Crow—each of them seems genuinely concerned that the paparazzi stalking has turned dangerous. The film reminds me that, while I'd like to feel the confidence or glamour or perfection that I perceive in celebrities,

I'm glad I'm not a famous star myself. There's the lack of privacy in your own home, the dangers of being chased by the flashing lights of the paparazzi, and the fact that tabloid photographers see it as their job to provoke a negative reaction at any given moment, since those are the pictures that sell for the big bucks.

Ann Helen Peterson, a media studies professor at Whitman College who writes the blog "Celebrity Gossip, Academic Style," explains in *Sellebrity* that today, stars aren't just actors or singers, they are commodities unto themselves. The product starts with raw material, in this case the human being, and is subsequently shaped by a public relations team (agent, manager, publicist, stylist—all those industry characters in *Entourage*), authorized publicity (television interviews, magazine covers, film or TV projects), and unauthorized publicity (tabloids, gossip sites, paparazzi photos). Once the human being is thrown into the fame machine and touched by all these outlets, you've got your final product. The Celebrity. And this machine is grander and more invasive today that it has ever been in the past.

It's tough to pity Sarah Jessica Parker or Jennifer Aniston for being too famous, which feels like part of their complaint during their *Sellebrity* interviews. As one *Us Weekly* reader tells the camera, "It comes with the job. You asked for this life." But they seem genuine in their assurances that the constant paparazzi abuse is not what they expected when they signed up for acting class twenty or thirty years ago.

The paparazzi's tendency to stalk stars as they leave the gym or carry groceries is indeed fairly modern, and the popularity of these photos is new to this century. It's not something that Sarah Jessica Parker could have seen in her future when she signed on to the cast of the TV show *Square Pegs* in 1982. In 1994, when *Friends* went on the air, tabloids weren't even close to what they've become today. It's *Us Weekly*, and its onetime editor in chief Bonnie Fuller, that turned celebrity journalism into the 24/7 watchdog we've come to know.

Though *Us Weekly* didn't captivate America until the turn of the century, the magazine has actually been in print since 1977. *Us*, then a monthly, was launched to compete with *People*, and I even subscribed back in the nineties, when it was basically a bi-weekly version of *Entertainment Weekly*. By the time Bonnie Fuller took over in 2002, the magazine had switched to a weekly, celebrity-focused format, but she was the one who introduced what has become the signature of the publication, the section that catapulted newsstand sales seemingly overnight: "Stars—They're Just Like Us!"

The history of that section, as told in *Sellebrity* by onetime *Us Weekly* news director Michael Lewittes, is fascinating. "[In 2002], a lot of the magazines would feature these glamorous shots of celebrities and at the time, *Us Weekly* wasn't doing that well. And so the only photos that *Us Weekly* could afford were those shots magazines wouldn't print. Bonnie snapped up those shots of celebrities taking out their garbage, picking up their kids. It was a home run for us." So basically, paparazzi stalkers and the Perez Hiltons of the world are largely due to the fact that *Us Weekly* was too broke for the good stuff.

To hear Bonnie Fuller tell it, she was trying to show the human side of celebrities. The intent of "Stars—They're Just Like Us!" was to show just that. But the side effect of this section is that readers feel *we* should be just like *them*. When bombarded by enough images of celebrities being "real people," somewhere deep down we start to ask: If they take out the trash, and so do I, then why don't I look that good doing it?

Sprinkled throughout the documentary are quotes from various artists, and there's one that really gets me: "Photography makes the world seem more available than it really is." Susan Sontag said it, and I think that's exactly what the recent tabloid revolution has done. These photos (not to mention reality TV shows and overnight YouTube stars) have made the fabulous lifestyles of the rich and famous seem, if just barely, available. Some might argue that's a good thing—suddenly we realize these celebrities aren't any better than we are, and fame and glamour are within our reach—but honestly, life might be easier if the message was the opposite. They're *Not* Like Us! They have money and access that's nearly impossible to come by! So don't compare yourself, because you're normal and they're not!

It might not sell magazines, but it would make it easier to accept those moments when you find yourself eating French fries on the couch without beating yourself up about it.

My overriding emotion while watching *Sellebrity*—as my magazine rack filled with *People*s and *Entertainment Weekly*s and *Vanity Fair*s sits next to the television—is guilt. This world that Jennifer and J.Lo and SJP are complaining about, I contribute to it. I click through gossip websites, and flip through *US Weekly* at the airport. I like to think I'm somehow better, because I spend more time on the "authorized" publicity, but I know I'm kidding myself. After all, this entire quest was inspired, and fueled, by those unauthorized photos. It's not the five-page spreads of Sarah Jessica in designer clothes that have me wanting to imitate her, it's the shots of her walking down a city street. And it's not any interview Jennifer Garner and Ben Affleck have done together that makes me long for their apparently perfect marriage. (I don't even think they've ever done any authorized publicity as a couple.) It's the photos of them holding hands at the park when they're just trying to enjoy a nice day with the family. The movie brings to light the commercialism of the celebrity universe. It reminds me that I am not merely influenced by the stars, but by the products that they've become and the magazines that deliver the goods.

* * *

On Sunday, though Matt isn't coming home until tomorrow, I watch the Patriots game by myself. This might be the most surprising development over the course of this entire project. But according to Jennifer Garner's sports theory, I need to watch five games to understand and get addicted. Four down.

* * *

This whole IVF thing is starting to stress me out. The other day I received my delivery of medication from the pharmacy. Forty-three boxes of medicine. Even more needles.

My apartment is now a pharmacy.

I haven't actually started any of the meds other than my birth control pill. I'll have to be on that for another week before I begin taking three self-administered shots a day. These shots will be responsible for stimulating my ovaries to produce multiple eggs, instead of the single one that develops during a typical menstrual cycle. During this period of stimulation, I'll be monitored via ultrasounds and blood tests to see that all is going well, and when it seems that all the eggs have reached a mature size (about eight to ten days after starting the shots) I'll take one final "trigger shot" to stimulate ovulation. At that point, I'll go in for a minor surgical procedure, during which they will retrieve all of my eggs and fertilize as many as they can with Matt's sperm. Then, another three to five days later, one or two of the resultant embryos will be transferred back into my uterus, and any other well-developed embryos will be frozen for possible later use.

It's a lot to take in. I've spoken with some friends and family about the process, but I haven't connected with anyone who's been through it herself. Instead, I continue to do myself the disservice of reading online message boards. I know they're meant to be helpful and supportive—and I know that plenty of women find comfort in these communities—but they just make me more anxious and get me more worked up. And even though I know better, and Matt has repeatedly told me to sign off the Internet for good, I'm like a junkie who can't give up her fix.

Clearly, my efforts to be Zen about the process are failing.

Matt has a fairly minimal tolerance for stress—his own, or other people's. He just doesn't believe in it. Despite my efforts to turn us into Ben and Jen 2.0, I'm nervous that this process will be hard on us. I'll be on edge; he'll be dismissive. I want him to be my rock, but I'm worried he'll think I'm being dramatic, and can feel myself getting preemptively mad at him for not understanding what I'm going through—even though this scenario only exists in my head, and hasn't yet played out in reality.

And then he proves me wrong.

It's Wednesday night, and Matt's just come home from work.

"I brought you something," he says.

I stare at him with confusion. I'm not proud of it, but I'm a bit of a snoop. It's not easy to pull a fast one on me, and Matt knows it. But no alarms have gone off on my surprise radar recently. I have no idea what Matt's getting at.

"This is just something to show my gratitude for everything you're about to go through in order to get us our baby," he says as he hands me a small jewelry box.

Inside is a pair of beautiful, small diamond stud earrings, something I've always wanted. "You should wear them whenever you start to get nervous or freaked out," Matt says. "And then you'll remember what we're doing this for."

Later, when I'm staring at my new jewelry, I remember something I read in a Jennifer Garner interview from a 2012 issue of *InStyle*. "[Ben] knows when to swoop in with the gesture," she said. "He's sweet that way."

Perhaps, in this one regard, I already have the celebrity life. I've definitely found my Ben.

CHAPTER SIX

JULIA ROBERTS'S SERENITY

"I'm so lucky to be crazy happy in my life. And I think it's not so much that I'm happier now than ever; it's that I'm more content. I'm in the harbor of my life." —O, The Oprah Magazine

"You can have very little from an outsider's point of view and feel deeply fulfilled. As long as you have a sense of fulfillment in your life then you do have it all. The older you get, the more fragile you understand life to be. I think that's good motivation for getting out of bed joyfully each day." —The Daily Mail

"I don't even know what a Facebook page looks like." —Access Hollywood

IVF makes life a little crazy. Shots need to be timed to a tee. Doctor visits, for at least a brief period, are almost daily. My ovaries are now the size of tennis balls (as opposed to their usual thumb-size), and I can feel them bouncing up and down whenever our car hits a speed bump. I'm more comfortable administering shots than I ever wanted to be, and have turned my thigh and stomach into pin cushions for my three nightly injections.

I'm glad we're doing these treatments—I certainly don't regret it—but it's not the most pleasant of experiences.

If there was ever a time to get a little Zen in my life, this is it.

———

I'm not sure why I think Julia Roberts is the most serene and peaceful celebrity out there. She doesn't run around screaming about Kabbalah, like Madonna, or touting transcendental meditation à la Oprah. She told *Elle* she is a practicing Hindu and goes to temple with her family to "chant and pray and celebrate," but she doesn't talk about her spirituality often. She did tell *The Telegraph* that she embraces meditation; that it's "a definite aspect of my family life and more than anything else, a constant state of gratitude is really the spiritual foundation of my daily life," but more often than not she keeps that personal information to herself.

In fact, it's not what she says that makes me associate Julia with serenity. It's what she doesn't say—she doesn't insert herself into tabloid drama or make the rounds on the celebrity circuit, at least not enough to find herself in the pages of *OK!* very often. Her interviews always steer into thoughtful territory, where she pontificates on peacefulness, fulfillment, contentedness, and family.

The fact that she lives in Taos, New Mexico, probably adds to her serene image, and it doesn't hurt that one of her most recent high-profile movie roles was playing Elizabeth Gilbert, queen of ashrams, in *Eat, Pray, Love*. When I imagine Julia on a typical afternoon, I picture her sitting in an adobe home, meditating below a giant Georgia O'Keefe painting with aromatherapy candles burning in the bathroom.

There's just something about her—that air of sheer satisfaction and peacefulness—that comes through in her every interview, photograph, or awards show appearance. And I want it.

After reading interview upon interview with Julia Roberts, I don't get nearly the same sense I did from those with Tina Fey or even Jennifer Garner. We could probably not be best friends. Julia seems far wiser, more calm, and more collected than I. She doesn't seem like the kind of woman whose mind is always racing to the next task. She has likely never been described as neurotic or frazzled or, on a good day, bubbly. She would never try to be like someone else in pursuit of her own happiness. She doesn't admit to feeling overwhelmed or indulging in a triannual sob, the very kind of admission that makes Tina so relatable.

But then, Julia Roberts is not relatable. Julia Roberts is Julia Roberts.

The thing about Julia is that she is *so* calm, *so* peaceful, *so* confident, that she drives some people crazy. A couple of years ago, I went on a girls' weekend with a group of friends and somehow talk turned to Julia. It turns out the majority of my pals can't stand her. They're turned off by her confidence. One of them couldn't stop quoting a *Family Guy* mockery of the superstar, during an episode where she is presenting at a telethon. "Hi, I'm Julia Roberts," *Family Guy* Julia says. "You know, a lot of people died in the tsunami. But don't worry, I didn't. I'll be here to entertain you and love my life for many many years to come. Me. *Meeeee. Meeeeeeeeeeeeee.*"

But I've never begrudged Julia her self-satisfaction. I admire it. Or envy it. I mean, she's Julia Roberts. Vivian Ward. Anna Scott. Erin Brockovich. How could she not feel good about being herself?

There's nothing I can do right now to change my daily shot regimen or trips to the doctor or my upcoming surgical procedure and the seemingly interminable two-week wait that will follow. But I can change the way I handle it. I can try to be at peace with it, and get through it in a state of calm rather than anxiety. I can try to be serene about the whole thing, and grateful that these fertility options exist, rather than anxious and frustrated that I couldn't just get my baby the old-fashioned way. I don't know that I can actually reach this state of serenity, but I can try.

To start, I want to incorporate daily meditation. Though Julia reportedly meditates, I don't know how often or for how long. Throughout this year I've tried to be pretty specific about emulating the regimens of my celebrity muses, but if there's any time when it makes sense to allow a little leeway, this month of serenity seems to be it. Part of being Zen is going easy on yourself and allowing yourself to make mistakes. It's leaning into changes without beating yourself up if you take a wrong turn. Serenity is listening to your body and mind and getting in touch with your internal needs and wants, and catering to that truth, rather than adhering to some externally dictated idea of what you *should* be doing.

At least, this is what my yoga teachers tell me.

I am not Hindu. I don't know much about chanting and praying, so despite Julia's example I'm not going to take that route. I have limited experience with meditation, but I've done enough in my years of yoga classes to have a general sense of how to breathe and clear my mind. I've collected various bits of meditation instruction, and I'm ready to use them. Sit in a comfortable cross-legged position. Be still. Take long breaths in and out. To clear your mind, count as you breathe in, count backward as you breathe out. I've heard teachers suggest mantras to repeat to yourself. ("Breathing in, I calm my body. Breathing out, I smile.") One even said to scroll the mantra in your mind's eye like a movie reel.

For my first day of at-home meditation, I pick and choose from these lessons to create my own customized process. Dr. Oz says a mere five minutes a day can add years to your life, so that sounds like a good place to start. Doing nothing but breathing in a dark room for five minutes will probably seem like forever.

Luckily, Matt isn't home for my first foray into meditation. He's not much of a spiritual guy, and he'd definitely think it strange to find his wife sitting on the floor in the corner of our pitch-black bathroom.

I figured it would be more relaxing to meditate in darkness, and our bathroom is the darkest place in the house, so here I am, cross-legged on a bathmat, trying to unwind as I cuddle up between our toilet and shower. I don't want to spend my entire first meditation wondering how many minutes are left, so I've downloaded a meditation app. "Meditation app" sounds like an oxymoron, but Mind, as it's called, is basically just a timer with a serene design. You set the rainbow-colored slider to anywhere between zero and sixty minutes, and once you tap to start the clock, Mind doesn't show you how much time you have left. It just says, "Relax. Focus on your breathing." After your designated meditation period is up, it plays two chimes. Very Zen.

As I suspected, five minutes is a long stretch of solitary silence. At least for a non-meditator. It's enough time for me to play out the plausible scenarios of the next month or so (the joy of pregnancy, the defeat of a failed transfer, the question of how we'll share the news either way) and the less plausible ones, too (what if we decide to transfer two embryos, both implant, and each one splits and I end up with two sets of identical twins? We don't have the closet space for six people). My yoga teachers—whom I clearly revere as the ultimate authorities on all things Zen, even though at least a couple of them are college kids who were certified in a course that involves more weight lifting than meditation—always say it's okay if your mind wanders during meditation, as long as you acknowledge it and bring your focus back to your breath. I notice my meandering thoughts and try to quiet them with a mantra, but by the time I've gotten to ". . . I calm my body" my mind has wandered back to the question of, if I do get pregnant, how will I break the news to my mom? My mother-in-law? Something cute like a baby book? Or more laid-back, like a casual mention in conversation?

Breathe, Rachel. Breathe.

There has been no chime, but I open one eye anyway, to peek at the timer. It doesn't say how many minutes I have left of my five, but there is a new message that has replaced "Relax. Focus on your breathing." Now my app reads, "You are almost done." It knows I'm getting antsy.

In another thirty seconds or so, my phone chimes. I don't feel especially serene, but I do feel like I've envisioned every possible IVF-related disaster scenario, so maybe meditation boosts my creative juices and stimulates my imagination. And there is the slightest sense of rejuvenation as I turn the lights on and re-steel myself for the rest of the day. Some quiet bathroom time is a nice brief respite, even if I didn't exactly find myself, as Elizabeth Gilbert once did, "in the palm of God."

Despite the only so-so results, I'm optimistic about continuing this serenity plan. If I've come up with all the worst-case scenarios today, maybe I've freed up my mind to calm itself tomorrow.

Meditation seems additionally appropriate right now because my usual head-clearing method is off-limits. Since kicking off this quest with Jennifer Aniston–inspired workouts, I've reignited my addiction to exercise. I don't spend time on the treadmill thinking, "Gee, this is fun, I can't wait to do another mile," but I feel more energized and healthy and upbeat, and also more calm and centered, on days when I boost my heart rate for an hour. It's a good way to start the day, too. Exercise gets me out of the house and forces me to break a sweat first thing, so I'm not tempted to stay in pajamas until 4 P.M.

One of the side effects of having enlarged ovaries is that exercise is forbidden. I can do gentle stretching, but my doctors say I must steer clear of any activity that will cause my ovaries to bounce for fear of ovarian torsion, a twisting of the ovaries that can be fairly dangerous. I'm not even allowed a brisk walk. Without my workouts, I've been missing the hour or so that helps me clear my head, calm my body, and start the process of feeling fabulous instead of frazzled. My hope is that meditation can take its place.

In a perfect world, my celebrity-driven day would look like this:

6:30 A.M: Wake up. Stretch, slowly adjust to daytime mode, read the morning headlines (news of both the worldly and entertainment variety). Eat healthy breakfast (oatmeal, eggs, or banana with almond butter).

7:30: Meditate. I'd like to get up to twenty minutes a day. Julia hasn't specified how long she meditates, but it seems that many celebrities—and scientists—say twenty is the magic number.

8:30–9:30: Workout #1. Running with strength training at my gym. In the last month I quit my part-time gig there—as the studio has gotten increasingly popular, the owners need more hours from employees, and I don't have time to work a six-hour shift. Instead, I negotiated a deal through which I write the studio's press materials—releases, member emails, promotional copy—in exchange for a discounted monthly rate. Win, win.

10:30: Head to the coffee shop or my office and get to work. At this point I should be in a real, put-together outfit. Ideally it would look cute without looking too matchy-matchy or thought-out. There's that effortless style that takes so much effort.

6:30: Pack up the computer, head to the kitchen to cook dinner. Fish tacos or salmon, rice and kale. Ideally a meal that would make both Gwyneth and Jennifer proud.

8:30: Watch TV while simultaneously doing workout #2. Pilates, yoga, Tracy Anderson Method. Mix and match for 30–45 minutes.

9:30: Spend some quality couple time with Matt. Jennifer Garner says you need to steal moments here and there. That's easier for us since we don't have kids, but sometimes those moments are just spent in front of *Top Chef* or a Patriots game. Other times, there's more intimacy involved.

10:30: Sneak in a little more work—blog posts, emails, whatever last-minute catch-up is leftover from the day.

11:30–12: Go to sleep. Start again tomorrow.

That is the perfect-world version of my day. The reality looks different. There are no hour-long workouts anymore. Except for the morning of our 7 A.M. RE appointment, I haven't woken up in the 6 A.M. hour in months. This will change should my baby dream come true, I know. But for now, I am what I am. I've come to believe that there are some things you can change about yourself and others you can't. Behavior can be altered—I can develop a workout routine, say, or a meditation practice—but I can't change my natural instincts. And my natural instincts are to sleep in the morning. I just can't make myself a morning person, no matter how hard I try. I will wake up if there's somewhere I have to be. If there's a doctor's appointment, or a workout class that I've already signed up for, I'll make it. But when a 6:30 wake-up call is simply to provide a peaceful hour of easing in to the day, my body won't do it. I've tried everything. I've put my alarm clock on the other side of the room. I've broken the snooze button. I've given myself a nighttime pep talk that tomorrow will be *the day*. None of it works. My semiconscious self cannot be changed, and at 6:30 A.M. my reaction to an alarm clock will remain the same: reset for 7:30, snooze for another fifteen minutes.

Similarly, no matter how much Gwyneth likes a good soy protein shake or foods made of seaweed, they will never appeal to my tastebuds. They make me gag, and they will never *not* make me throw up a little bit in my mouth. That's just who I am. But I'm getting better at distinguishing the bits of celebrity behavior that I can adopt from the natural instincts I'll never be able to change. For example, I can avoid eating fried food (behavior) but I can't stop loving the taste (natural instinct). Those celebrities who claim they don't watch what they eat, they simply crave fresh veggies from the farmer's market? That will never be me. I think anyone who says she only craves fresh fruit is a liar, but that's probably my junk-food lover's bias.

* * *

There is a lot of speculation out there that Julia Roberts used in vitro fertilization to conceive her twins, Phinnaeus and Hazel. Julia has never addressed the issue herself, so I don't know if I share the company of the ultimate Hollywood Royalty, but I certainly wouldn't be surprised. IVF and other treatments have become so common these days that I often assume anyone with fraternal twins went through fertility measures.

I still don't know if twins are in my future, but I got a call today, Tuesday, from my nurse telling me it's time. My eggs are ripe and ready for the taking. The plan, she says, is to take my trigger shot—the injection of medicine that will trigger my follicles to release the eggs—tonight, and do my egg retrieval on Thursday afternoon.

"Set your alarm," the nurse says. "You need to take the shot at 3 A.M., and your procedure will be at 3 P.M. Thursday."

Three A.M. it is. I run around the apartment, setting four different alarm clocks, still shocked at the idea that in two days' time I could have little embryos growing in a dish.

At 2:45, the first alarm goes off. I start rousing Matt. This shot is different—bigger—than the shots I've been taking for the last couple of weeks, so we need to watch a video tutorial on how it's done. Most of the previous shots I've administered myself, but this one goes straight into the butt cheek, rather than the thigh or stomach, which means Matt will be playing nurse.

As Matt preps himself for giving the injection—he might be more nervous than I am—I try to channel my meditative state. Deep breaths, calm the mind. I'm glad I've been practicing this, because now I really need it. If you can stay centered while your husband shoves a giant needle in your butt, you've pretty much mastered serenity.

* * *

The next week passes in a blur that is neither glamorous nor anywhere near perfect. Any attempts to be a well-dressed, fit, healthy, Zen version of myself go out the window after a minor surgery that confines me to the couch for five days. Despite the literature's assurance that I would be back at work the day after my egg retrieval, I was in pretty serious pain for three days, and significant discomfort for another two.

When you're so bloated that you can hardly stand up, things like cooking or even getting dressed feel completely out of reach.

But I'm not giving myself a hard time about it. This may be a quest about gaining control and attaining that I've-got-it-together feeling, but the flip side to actually moving toward that goal is that the days when you abandon any pretense of togetherness feel indulgent rather than lazy. Six months ago, this weekend's complete disregard for anything but television might have felt like another day where I failed to get anything crossed off my to-do list. But now it feels like a well-deserved treat. I've often found this to be true: When you're in pursuit of one thing, you develop an increased appreciation for its opposite. During the year I spent searching for new friends, I learned the value of alone time. When I spend day after day checking items off the "celebrity perfection checklist," allowing myself to abandon the structure is oh-so-sweet. As a result, Matt and I make no apologies for the days between my egg retrieval and transfer, which we spend watching the first two seasons of *Homeland*.

Watching Carrie Mathison fall apart really puts your own issues of control and perfectionism in perspective.

On the day of the transfer, the embryologist tells us we have six mature fertilized embryos. We won't be transferring all six into my uterus—no one's trying to be the Gosselins here—but it's good to know we'll have some backup in the freezer if this transfer doesn't take.

Matt and I are in our full scrub regalia when Dr. E comes in.

"Everything looks great," she says. "But the embryos aren't as far along as I expected them to be, so it's not as clear cut regarding whether to transfer one or two."

I feel my heart jump. Or maybe it's my stomach dropping.

In our first meeting, Dr. E told us she would likely recommend transferring only one embryo when the time came. Our chances of success would be so high that transferring two wouldn't necessarily increase our odds of getting a baby, she said, and one baby is always a more optimal outcome than twins, for both medical and sanity purposes.

Now our chart is telling a different story, and for the first time the reality hits that we could actually be parents to two babies at once.

I said I want to be like Julia or Sarah Jessica, both mothers of twins, but I'm not sure I'm ready for this.

"It's up to you," Dr. E says. "Have you guys discussed whether you're okay with the possibility of twins?"

I look at Matt, who has a huge smile on his face. He looks like he's about to burst out laughing.

"Sure," I say. "We're okay with twins. Better two than none."

* * *

I picked the right time to focus on serenity. After a smooth transfer, Matt and I are in what the fertility clinic calls the Two-Week Wait. There are two embryos hanging out in my uterus, but whether or not they will implant is anybody's guess. At the time of our transfer, I pushed the embryologist for more odds. Given our specific situation, he put the chances of one baby at 65 percent, and twins at 35. Sixty-five percent is even better than where we started, but it's hardly a guarantee. And now we have two weeks to kill before I can go in for my blood test to get the big news.

"Don't take a pregnancy test," Dr. E told me before I left my transfer. "If you test too early, you could get a false negative, and if you still have hormones from your trigger shot in your system, it could give a false positive. Don't do it."

I could feel Matt's stern glare on the side of my face. "Don't take a test," he told me on the ride home. "I know waiting will be nearly impossible for you, but it's a bad idea. Listen to the doctor." I agreed, begrudgingly, but now that we're back home, just waiting around for the biggest news of our lives, I'm tempted.

Instead, I try to recenter myself. I go back to channeling Julia. Now is the time to relax, calm my mind, and be patient. In an interview with Oprah, Julia once said, "What happens is going to happen, whether you're sitting by the phone anxious and worried about it or not." Of course, she was talking about getting box office numbers and I'm talking about getting a baby, but the same principle applies.

In an attempt to resist scouring the Internet for every article entitled "Early Signs of Pregnancy" and scanning my body for sore breasts, implantation cramps, or an extrasensitive sense of smell, I'm focusing on living my new life. Meditating, writing, cooking—whatever will keep me busy, distracted, and make the time pass.

It's not easy. The handful of friends and family I've told about our IVF process have been checking up on me fairly regularly, which is kind but also keeps this maybe-baby on the brain. Then there's the fact that I'm currently taking some five different medicines daily. But mostly, I can't stop my mind from wandering to all the hypothetical scenarios that could play out in the coming weeks.

I've upped my daily meditation time to ten minutes. My goal was to do it first thing in the morning (see: perfect day) but I tend to work it in closer to noon for a midday break. Now, on top of the mere fact that ten minutes of silence feels interminable (I peek at the clock about three times a session), my attention is being drawn away from my breath and to the various body parts that are working overtime. After about seven minutes of sitting cross-legged, I feel it in my hips. And my back. I've never been so aware of my poor posture as I am now, since sitting up straight for ten minutes feels like a strenuous back workout. If one of the goals of meditation is to get in touch with your body, it's working. But the tightness and twinging and sheer discomfort of the meditative position—especially when I'm still as bloated as Violet Beau-regard—is making it tough to clear my mind.

Focusing on work has been the hardest part. I'm trying to be productive in my writing and reporting, but I can barely sit still long enough to string a sentence together. There's a lot of staring at blank pages, typing two words, googling a research statistic I want to include in an article and instead finding myself on Baby-Center's due date calculator. It's become a reflex. I intend to go to ScienceDaily to look up a health study for a story, and instead I find myself staring at a screen that says, "your embryo is smaller than a poppy seed." How did I get here?

I recently read a blog post on the Harvard Business Review network by Peter Bregman, author of *18 Minutes: Find Your Focus, Master Distraction, and Get the Right Things Done,* about how meditation can make a person more productive. He explains that with a daily twenty-minute meditation practice, he's honed his ability to recognize mind wandering and bring his focus back to his breath—a skill that has also improved his ability to tune out distractions at work. "Sometimes not following through on some-thing you want to do is a problem, like not writing that proposal you've been procrastinating on . . . but other times, the problem is that you do follow through on something you don't want to do. Like speaking instead of listening or playing politics instead of rising above them. Meditation teaches us to resist the urge of that counterproductive follow-through." My personal distraction comes more in the form of People.com than office politics, but I can relate to what Bregman is saying. Why do I click over to Facebook when I know I should be writing? Or, more pressingly, why do I continue to look up the due date of my hypothetical baby when I need to be doing just about anything else?

Research supports Bregman's contention. A study from the University of Washington found that those with experience meditating "were able to stay on task longer and were less distracted," according to *USA Today*. Meditation, the study authors say, is like exercise. "It strengthens your attention muscle."

This is exactly what I need. Until now, I hadn't made the connection between my Tina Fey work quest and the one for Julia's serenity. But the two are clearly linked. The more Julia-calm I am, the more Tina-productive I'll be. The meditators among us are less likely to get overwhelmed, more likely to handle stress and chaos calmly, and have an ability to focus that currently feels completely out of my grasp. Were I to have Julia's peace and serenity I could tune out the baby anxiety and focus on the task at hand, be it writing, cooking, or even sleeping.

Since incorporating Julia into my web of celebrity muses, I've given up social media. Ms. Roberts doesn't bother with it. I learned this a couple of weeks ago when I got an email from a friend: "I saw Julia Roberts do a TV interview in which she said she doesn't know what a Facebook page looks like and neither do her kids. She said it so serenely and wisely, I was like, 'NO FACEBOOK! I WANT TO BE LIKE JULIA!'"

Cutting out social media has eliminated my primary method of procrastination. Scrolling status updates and reading tweets are my go-to I-should-be-at-my-computer-but-I-don't-actually-want-to-write distractions. Now that I'm on a Facebook ban, I spend a lot of time staring into space. I can't get work done, but I can't distract myself with social media, so I just sit there, paralyzed, as if I've been banned from all social interaction rather than just the random photos of third-degree acquaintances that I usually consume online. The ability to refocus on work would be helpful.

When I got that email from my friend, I looked up the interview in question. Julia was talking to *Access Hollywood*'s hosts when she explained that, "I don't even know what a Facebook page looks like. I think twittering is when Danny comes home from work and I . . . [*giggle, giggle*]."

It's a line that makes me hate her and want to be her all at the same time. Really? You've *never* seen a Facebook page? That's something a person has to actively try to avoid. You didn't even see *The Social Network*? It was nominated for Best Picture! And you're Julia Roberts!

But I also feel as my friend did. *I wish I had never seen a Facebook page! What am I doing wasting hours perusing boring status updates? I want to be serene and wise, too!*

It's a common conflict when it comes to celebrity crushes, this strange love-hate relationship. We want to be like them, but we also sort of want to punch them for being so ostentatiously perfect. They make us doubt ourselves, and yet we keep coming back for more. Like one pal told me when I explained to her my celebrity life plans:

"I love that idea! I sort of despise Goop for the feeling of inadequacy it unlocks inside of me." And yet she still subscribes and reads it every Thursday.

When I tell friends that emulating Julia means going on a Facebook fast because she's never seen it for herself, or that she claims to not even know what Twitter is, they roll their eyes. She and Gwyneth have a similar thing going—an enigmatic pull that even their fans don't understand.

But I don't need to comprehend it. The point of this whole quest is to follow the examples of those who seem to feel the way I'd like to feel, the celebrities who present themselves to the world in a way I'd like to present myself, and see if it makes me feel glamorous, together, and happier. It does, in some ways, amount to becoming a sheep—blindly following without always considering why I'm doing what I'm doing. I've tried to remember to ask myself if the actions I'm taking will in fact make me happier, but sometimes I just don't know. Will cutting out Facebook improve my life? It's unclear, but the answer will come in time. We can't always be sure of what will make us happy, and I've been surprised enough in the past to avoid writing anything off too quickly.

And so I've cut out Facebook.

This social media fast can be added to the list of developments that have Matt especially excited. (Others include cooking and New England Patriots fandom.) Though he has seen a Facebook page or two, he's never signed up for the social network himself. He's not on Twitter, Instagram, Foursquare, or any other site that has any kind of feed. Technology has never been his strong suit—in college, when everyone else was making plans via Instant Message, he refused to get a screen name. "I'm too sarcastic," he told me back then. "My sense of humor would be misunderstood."

At this point, I think Matt's social network absence is part of his persona. If he's held out this long, why sign up now? Maybe it's too late to get on the bandwagon, though he'd never say that's the reason. "The people I want to communicate with, I'll communicate with over phone or email," he tells me when I ask why he's so anti-Facebook. "Why do I need to know what everyone's doing all the time?"

I'm on Facebook, Twitter, and Instagram. I play Words with Friends. I would never call myself a social media addict, but this fast has forced me to reconsider my relationship with the sites. I rarely post on Facebook, and 95 percent of what I do post is work-related—blog posts, book updates, speaking events. The other 5 percent are pop culture links—a *Grantland* article on why everyone should be watching *Parenthood*, a YouTube video of the *Party of Five* opening credits, a poster for the Austin TV Fest. The main purpose of my social media use is to keep tabs on other people—to look at baby and wedding pictures, find interesting links, or see what fabulous vacations other people are taking while I'm sitting at my desk not working. The catch is that, usually, these people aren't even my friends. Most of my real, close friends, are like me—non-posters. We creep around, looking at what others have to say. The people I'm keeping tabs on are long-lost neighbors, ex-coworkers, and kids I went to high school with fifteen years ago. Like Matt said, the friends I want to talk to, I talk to. What I'm doing here on Facebook is simply wasting time.

Still, giving it up has been one of the toughest tasks of this year. I don't feel more Zen for having abstained from status updates. If anything I feel out of touch, as if there's a party raging online and I'm missing out.

The hardest part of my Facebookless days, though, isn't this feeling of disconnectedness. It's that I'm so used to typing those letters into my web browser when I'm looking to procrastinate that my fingers seem to act independently of my brain. When I'm looking for a mindless time suck, a way of putting off doing the work that takes focus, I switch to autopilot. I don't realize what I've done until it's too late to stop myself.

But serenity is about mindfulness, so each time I end up on Facebook or Twitter or Instagram, I remember, refocus, and shut down my web browser. My inner Julia will thank me.

* * *

Tonight, Oxygen is running a Julia Roberts mini-marathon. First *Eat, Pray, Love,* then *Pretty Woman.* The films are nothing alike. Julia's characters might as well be exact opposites. *Eat, Pray, Love* was critically panned and a box office disappointment while *Pretty Woman* is arguably the most popular romantic comedy of all time. But even in *Eat, Pray, Love* there's something magnetic about her. Julia can carry a film.

Pretty Woman came out in 1991. Julia was all of twenty-one years old. I can't imagine she was the serene, contented soul I take her to be today. But to hear her tell it, the industry was different back then. Perfection wasn't the standard, and celebrities weren't constantly being scrutinized. In an interview with Oprah, she explained her take on the new marketing machine: "I don't dislike it. I just don't think I'm very good at it. I like everybody being nice to everybody. And there's an element that's so unkind, so mean-spirited. It used to be more polite. I couldn't be an ingenue today, because the business has changed. I remember when you could dress for a premiere just by putting on a cute top. Now you have to be perfect and fabulous in every way, or you're ridiculed."

That interview was done in 2003, only a year after *Us Weekly* took off and celebrity tabloid journalism became the booming business it is today. A decade later, those expectations of perfection and fabulousness are even higher. It's not good enough to look amazing only on the red carpet. You're just as likely to be photographed pumping gas as you are attending a movie premiere. "Show business itself has changed and it's not treated in a treasured, magical way anymore," Julia told the *Daily Mirror* in 2010. "Everybody wants to know how the tricks are done and what the actors do twenty-four hours a day and it kind of takes a little bit of the fun away from the experience of going to a movie."

In the twenty-plus years since *Pretty Woman* was released, Julia and show business have both changed, and it seems as if they've moved in opposite directions. She's gotten older, wiser, and has strayed far from the gossip scene. There was a time, in the early nineties, when Julia called off her wedding to Kiefer Sutherland only days before they were to be married, and rumors flew that she was a terror on set and had a drug problem. It was the story of the summer back in 1991, and in an interview with *Entertainment Weekly* she explained what she wanted for her life going forward: "I want to be freed from this imprisonment of photographers outside my house, of people jumping out at me in the dark, simply because I am an Everygirl. I am just a girl, and I am 24 years old, and I just want to have, like, this nice life and be able to run around and laugh and have fun and not sit hunched down with a hat on all the time and my hair down in my face. I want to be able to look up and see everything instead of always feeling like I have to hide. . . ."

It seems as if she's achieved that—taking up residence in New Mexico probably helped—and the more I think about Julia, and this whole serenity pursuit, the more elusive it feels. You can see if someone has a fit body or a great wardrobe. You can read a cookbook or watch a food show for proof that someone knows her way around a kitchen. Peacefulness isn't quite so tangible. There's no visual evidence, no recipe to follow. Serenity is internal. Only an individual can know if she's achieved a state of contentedness, and it's that quality—maybe more than any other—that attracts us to certain stars. If celebrity appeal were just about glamorous looks, then photos of stars walking the dog in sweats would be far less interesting. But it's that air of have-it-all-ness that we peons flock to and crave, and that comes from confidence, which in turn comes from contentedness. It's hard to exude self-assurance when you aren't pleased with who you are, and, while not all celebrities who seem confident also seem serene, I'd argue that those are the ones we most admire and want to emulate. (This could be why so many women are turned off by Kristen Stewart. She seems so uncomfortable in her own skin. It might also explain the growing anti–Anne Hathaway movement. She seems to try too hard.) While Julia represents the pinnacle of peacefulness, all the women I've studied over the course of this quest seem similarly unflappable.

* * *

With a week to go before we get our baby news, my friend Sara comes into town for a visit from New York City. She's in Chicago for work, but the timing couldn't be better. "I will give your hormoned-up body lots of hugs!" she tells me in an email. "If all goes smoothly, I'm excited to tell your kid(s) I was there the week you got pregnant with them. I will have known them from the very start!"

Sara and I have been best friends since we were ten so it's fitting that she would be the one to "know" my child (or children) the longest. We stay up late chatting and watching bad reality TV, eat delicious meals, and go to a movie. Though meditation is great, there's nothing like having a best friend around for the purposes of healthy distraction. And I think Julia would agree. She talks plenty about her best friend, Paige, whom she has known for more than twenty-five years and who often accompanies her on talk show interviews or other appearances.

When it comes to serenity, or maybe sanity, there's nothing like a good girls' weekend to help you get peace.

Even if Sara and I do spend half the time considering potential baby names.

* * *

Once Sara leaves, I've got only a couple of days left before the big blood draw. I'm proud to say I've withstood the lure of the pregnancy test—probably because I threw them all out as a preventative measure.

Despite daily meditation, I'm having plenty of trouble remaining calm or focused. But I'm enjoying the lack of Facebook, which has been a surprise. While the site certainly acts as a good distraction when I'm antsy, it doesn't have a calming effect, which is what I need right now. Facebook leaves me with envy of other people's vacation and baby photos, and makes me feel generally creepy for the amount I suddenly know about random connections' lives. In the past, I've clicked over to Facebook, despite knowing that I didn't particularly enjoy it, at the cost of productivity and sometimes sanity—which I'm pretty sure is the definition of addiction. (As it turns out, there is an actual Facebook Addiction Scale, developed by the psychology faculty at the University of Bergen in Norway. You have to rate yourself on a scale of "very rarely" to "very often" for statements like "You spend a lot of time thinking about Facebook or planning use of Facebook" and "You become restless or troubled if you are prohibited from using Facebook." I don't fit the addict profile, but I'd like to be much closer to a "clearly has no attachment to Facebook" description than I am.) Now that I've trained myself not to automatically pull up the site for no reason, I'm better off.

Symptom-wise, I feel fine. No nausea, no unusual fatigue. I know it's still early to feel something, but that doesn't stop me from poking myself in the boobs every now and then to see if it hurts. And then it does, and I can't decide if I'm sore because I'm pregnant or because I've spent the last thirty seconds poking myself.

You can see why I need answers.

My mom says that when she got pregnant with me, she knew the next day. "I could just tell," she says, "something was different." I'm pretty sure that's revisionist history, as women don't always conceive the moment they do the deed (months of fertility reading has taught me that sperm can hang out for up to five days waiting to fertilize an egg) and it's not like everything suddenly changes in the moment of fertilization, but her words still haunt me.

"I feel exactly the same," I tell Matt two nights before we'll find out. "Nothing about me feels pregnant."

"But you've never been pregnant, so you don't even know what it feels like," Matt, ever the lawyer, counters. "You need to stop putting so much stock into your mother's whole 'just knowing' story. It's ridiculous."

What I really need to do, I think, is brace myself for the possibility that I'm not pregnant. The odds are in our favor, but who knows how this science will play out. We could get unlucky, and perhaps if I prepare for it, and plan how I will cope, I can soften what will be a devastating blow.

My first form of self-preservation has been to tell no one—not Sara, not my mom, no one—the date of our pregnancy test. I've given a vague "in a couple of weeks, we haven't scheduled it yet" answer when asked. In the event that the results are negative, I want time to sit with the information, cope, and break the news to others when I'm ready. Matt and I have agreed that this is the best course of action. On the flip side, if the news is good, we'll be able to celebrate between us, and still surprise our parents when the time comes.

The second part of preparing for the worst comes directly from the Julia Roberts playbook. In a 2012 interview with the *Daily Mail,* Julia explained a bit more how she reaches her state of Zen: "You can have very little from an outsider's point of view and feel deeply fulfilled. As long as you have a sense of fulfillment in your life, then you do have it all. . . . I think that's good motivation for getting out of bed joyfully each day." What I need, it seems, is a clear and strong sense of fulfillment in my life—even without a baby. If I can feel satisfied already, before I even go in for a pregnancy test, then maybe I'll be less negatively affected by a disappointing outcome.

Part of the reason I launched this quest in the first place was that I was feeling unfulfilled—I was sluggish and a little grumpy, and I knew I wanted to feel more conquer-the-world fabulous, I just wasn't sure where to start. As I've systematically tackled different aspects of my life over the past months, I've increased that sense of fulfillment. I'm more pleased and more content in areas where I once felt lacking, and I'm sure the serene, Zen, Julia way of facing this pregnancy quest would be to focus on all that I do have, rather than the one thing I don't.

In interviews, Julia talks plenty about gratitude, and maybe that's what I need to concentrate on right now. If I can remind myself of all the reasons I'm lucky—and I'm aware that I am, in fact, quite lucky—then maybe, as Julia says, I'll "have it all."

This is another Matt-approved exercise. He often gets annoyed at me when I lose perspective. No matter what my complaint, he will counter with the starving children in Africa to remind me how good we have it. The argument usually continues with me explaining that *that* problem, while certainly more severe than my own, doesn't invalidate my feelings, and we end up agreeing to disagree.

But, of course, I am grateful. I have a fantastic marriage, a supportive family, great friends, and the career I've wanted since I was a little girl. I have food on the table and a roof over my head, and the ability to pay for both. There are plenty of little things to be grateful for too: my shower radio, the café on my corner with free Wi-Fi, the checkout guy at the grocery store who lent me $2 once when I forgot my wallet and was desperate for a Diet Coke and Luna bar. I'm grateful that we identified our fertility problem when we did, that we found a doctor we trust, that we have four more frozen embryos should we need them, and that we have access to IVF in the first place. I'm grateful that I sleep through the night without getting up to pee and that Matt doesn't snore and that there's a cupcake shop on my corner.

The science of gratitude is very hip these days. Gratitude journals are especially hot—one study found that writing in a gratitude journal only once a week can have a significant effect over the course of a few months. Write down five sentences a week, one for each of five things you're grateful for, and you'll be happier, more optimistic, and more physically fit. I've tried to keep many journals in the course of my life, and I've never been able to maintain one for long, so I already know this practice isn't for me. But given that I'm looking for a more immediate hit of thankfulness, I decide to make a list. If I enumerate every single thing I'm grateful for in my entire life, right now, in one fell swoop, maybe it will give me a small buffer for the big pregnancy test. It won't erase all the sadness should things go badly, but it could mitigate the pain.

Maybe.

It's certainly worth a shot.

Thirty minutes later I have written a list of fifty-one things I'm grateful for. The first: my marriage. The last: my Snuggie. It doesn't make me want a baby any less, but it certainly helps remind me that I have a pretty great life, and a lot to be thankful for.

* * *

The time has come. I've meditated, I've been grateful, and I've cut out potentially toxic outside influences like Facebook and Twitter. I am as serene as I can get, and it's time for a blood test.

As I roll up my sleeve, the nurse wishes me luck. She tells me I can expect a call in the afternoon from my nurse, though I expect it will be Dr. E who delivers the news. She slaps a Band-Aid on my very tired vein (IVF includes a lot of blood work) and that's it. Five minutes, in and out, and now a few more hours of waiting.

I go to my favorite diner and eat my favorite omelet. I divert my eyes as I walk past the baby store on the way back to my car. I spend the morning cooking a chocolate chip pumpkin bread loaf, which ends up crumbling to pieces when I try to take it out of the pan but at least still tastes good when eaten crumb by crumb.

At 1:09 my phone rings. I come the closest I ever have to a heart attack and grab my cell.

It's my mom.

I call Matt at work. "Hello?" I can hear the anticipation in his voice.

"Whatcha doin'?" I say, making clear I have no news.

"You are not allowed to call again until you have something important to say," he tells me.

"Fair enough. Bye." I hang up the phone.

At 2:45 the phone rings again.

"Rachel? It's Dr. E."

"Hi! How are you?" I don't know why I'm trying to play it cool. We both know what I'm thinking.

"I'm great," she says. "You're pregnant."

CHAPTER SEVEN

JESSICA ALBA'S PREGNANCY

"At the end of the day I am so tired I can't function or speak and my eyes glaze over; but this pregnancy has seriously mellowed me out, which is nice. I've been going, going, going for so long, it feels nice not to have to take things so seriously."
—FitPregnancy

"If you are sporting a pregnant belly, it's better to show it than to hide it. If you look in the mirror and you look really wide and frumpy, then you're going to appear really wide and frumpy. The more figure-forming your clothes, even though you have more curves, the better. I like long, thin sweaters that kind of hide my hips and my booty, so there's not a huge emphasis on how big they're getting."
—Latina

"Before I had kids, I was very responsible and serious. I used to be all about controlling my environment; everything had to be just so. Now my idea of perfection is different. You can label bins and have a place for stuff, but when the kids go into the playroom you're not going to say, 'We can't paint, because how are we going to clean up?'"
—InStyle

I have taken five pregnancy tests in the last week. After ten months of peeing on sticks, I didn't believe they actually worked until five days ago. But there it was, a faint but discernible plus sign. The other four were more out of excitement than disbelief. Is a baby really in there? According to ClearBlue, EPT, and First Response, it is.

In the world of psychology, there's research that says achieving a goal won't necessarily make you happier. It's the act of pursuing the goal, some scientists say, that provides the best results. Buy a big house, land that promotion, or lose those last five pounds—you'll be pleased for a moment, but you'll recalibrate to your same basic happiness level pretty quickly. Working toward a goal might be invigorating, but the moment of achievement can feel anticlimactic. Even this celebrity-inspired quest has yielded a similar conclusion thus far. It's hard to imagine I'll ever achieve my version of perfection, but simply making progress propels me to keep at it.

When it comes to pregnancy, though, reaching my goal is as thrilling as I always expected it to be. Knowing there's a baby growing inside me, I am happy. Matt is happy. We're both in a state of ecstatic shock.

Elation, it turns out, can be paralyzing. I used to think it was only the opposite—melancholy, or at least lethargy—that would drive a person to take to the couch, but now I know better. If my nerves made it hard for me to focus last month, the pregnancy news has made it impossible now. I'm still not allowed to work out, I'm too antsy to meditate, I certainly can't focus on getting any valuable writing done. I have a one-track mind, and while I can hardly wipe the smile off my face, I've fallen off the wagon when it comes to my life of control, glamour, and have-it-all-together-ness.

For a couple of weeks, I embrace it. I'm pregnant! Bring on the fries! I'm taking this opportunity to eat everything in sight. Cookies? Yes, please. Cheese? Don't mind if I do. Pizza? I'll take two slices, thanks. At a family brunch one morning, everyone orders egg white omelets—I opt for French toast. Everything is fair game, and I make no apologies for indulging.

We haven't told many people that I'm pregnant yet, just some family and close friends, but I've overheard Matt discussing my food choices over the phone. "Her cravings? Mostly fried food and chocolate."

I decide not to tell my husband that it's too early for actual pregnancy cravings. These are called "I haven't eaten Chicken McNuggets in three years and I'm finally not on a diet" cravings, but I'll let him believe what he wants.

Two weeks after the blood test, Matt and I go to Dr. E's office for an ultrasound. It's a big moment. We'll hopefully get to see a heartbeat, and we'll definitely find out how many babies are in there.

"How are you feeling?" Dr. E asks.

"I'm good. Excited! I still can't believe it," I tell her. I explain that I've been lucky so far—no nausea, just some fatigue. My mom had no morning sickness, and Dr. E says it's usually hereditary, so I could be in the clear.

When the technician turns the ultrasound screen toward Matt and me, we can see it. One blinking dot.

"There's the heartbeat," Dr. E says. It's pretty crazy. There's hardly anything to see—the embryo is the size of a lentil, and onscreen it looks like a tiny bean-shaped blob, but it's our blob.

"Where's the other one?" I ask. We've spent the last two weeks steeling ourselves for twins.

"Looks like that's it," she says.

Matt and I exchange a look of surprise.

"Believe me, you'll be grateful," she says. "In the middle of the night when you are both up because of one screamer, you'll be glad there aren't two."

On the way home we stop off at our favorite deli. I get an everything bagel with chive cream cheese and a bag of chips, and contemplate a black-and-white cookie. Matt, the healthy eater who usually gives me the stink eye when I go too crazy on junk food, tells me to go for it. "You're pregnant, baby. Live it up!"

A few more days like this and I start to feel gross. Happy and excited, but gross. Pregnancy itself is not to blame. Yes, it's making me so tired I have to take two-hour naps in the late afternoon, but otherwise I'm feeling healthy. The grossness comes from the same place it did at the beginning of the year—the elastic waistbands that have reemerged from the closet, the excessively snoozed alarm clock, and the total disregard for the schedule or order I've introduced into my life over the last six months.

I'm reminded of one of the reasons I originally started this quest: Having a baby, I reasoned, will turn life as I know it upside down. A person has to relinquish some control when much of her life is dictated by the eating and sleeping schedule of a newborn. The better I can feel going into parenthood, both physically and mentally, the more likely I am to keep it together when there's a new addition to our family. That's not to say I will be like Angelina Jolie, strutting the streets with a clan of children while looking as if I just stepped off a glamour shoot and haven't lost a moment of sleep, but maybe I'll give myself a fighting chance. I wouldn't exactly *mind* looking like Heidi Klum or Halle Berry, at the park with my kid while emanating that celebrity-glow that seems to call to paparazzi like high-pitched whistles to dogs.

I'm not saying it's going to happen. I'm just saying I wouldn't fight it.

After two weeks off the wagon, I've gained five pounds. My doctor says some of it is bloat from the IVF meds, but I'm not so sure. Two weeks without a vegetable can pack on weight. From what I've read in the baby books, a woman is supposed to gain about two to four pounds in her first trimester. That's the first thirteen weeks of pregnancy. I've already gained five, in half that time.

Baby weight, I know, is different for everyone. Different women, different bodies, blah blah blah. I call it the Jessica Scale. Some women are more Jessica Alba, others are more Jessica Simpson.

There's nothing wrong with either of them. They both gained a good amount of weight during their pregnancies, and gave birth to healthy, adorable children. Ms. Alba has said she put on more than fifty-five pounds with her first daughter, Honor, though less with number two, Haven. Ms. Simpson reportedly gained about seventy pounds during her first pregnancy. But that fifteen-pound difference isn't what separates them. From their appearances in magazines and TV interviews while expecting, it seemed like Jessica Simpson gained all over, while Jessica Alba was nearly all belly.

Given my pear-shaped body type, I'll probably be more Simpson than Alba. I don't expect to be one of those women who looks like she swallowed a basketball. But I want to be Alba on the Jessica Scale for more than just her body. Simpson has admitted that she wanted to let loose and have fun during her first pregnancy, but as a result, she told Jay Leno, "I didn't really make any healthy good decisions." I want to enjoy pregnancy, but I'd like to do it the healthy Alba way. I want her whole mom-to-be demeanor. Jessica Alba made clear in interviews that carrying her babies was the best time of her life—she was relaxed and happy and poised and cool. She was in control, she said, making decisions for the kids rather than for the fun of finally letting go. She portrayed those nine months as a lifestyle to covet.

Somehow Jessica Alba made pregnancy look stylish, chill, en-lightening, and even sexy. Twice.

If an amazing body were all it took to make a specific celebrity the pinnacle of pregnancies, that role could be filled by any number of A-listers (Natalie Portman, Reese Witherspoon, Beyoncé, to name a few). But Jessica Alba has turned motherhood into a job. Not just her off-the-clock, being-a-mom-is-a-full-time-job job, but her business. It wasn't enough to be a stunner with a baby bump, one who gave interviews that made pregnancy sound like a nine-month state of bliss. She also became so passionate about exposing her kids to only healthy, safe, and sustainable products that she started The Honest Company, making "baby items that are cute and eco-friendly," she told *LA Confidential*.

Reading interviews with Jessica Alba, I start to think that maybe I've got it all wrong. Maybe having a baby won't turn my life upside down. Maybe it will turn me into a wise, relaxed, nothing-can-bother-me-there's-a-baby-in-my-belly ball of confidence.

With Jessica as my guide, I'm getting back to work. Dr. E said I'm finally free to exercise, so I've signed up for my workout classes. I'm also returning to the meditation, planting my butt in front of my writing, wearing something that isn't necessarily made of flannel, and Alba-ing this pregnancy out of the park.

Step one: Go natural. How can I be Jessica without Jessica's products? From what I can tell, the Honest Company sells baby products—diapers, shampoos, lotions, the like—but not much for pregnancy. In an interview with TheStir.com, Jessica did give this advice: "Anything that's petroleum-based, you want to avoid. And a lot of toxic chemicals are hidden in our fragrances . . . So unless you know that it's something that is safe and nontoxic, it's probably best to just avoid."

She also mentions phthalates and BPA, and I start to feel like I need a chemistry degree to understand what I can and can't use. The maternity store nearest to my apartment carries a brand called Erbaviva, which is labeled both natural and organic, so I start with that. I buy a sample kit—mini lip balm, stretch mark cream and oil, and milk bath. The package runs me $30. Not outrageous, but steep for such tiny travel-size bottles. Cheaper than Crème de la Mer, I guess. (If there is one celebrity beauty must-have I wish I could indulge in, it's Crème de la Mer moisturizer. It seems that every celebrity, including Ms. Alba, swears by the stuff. But at $275 for 2 ounces—even Jessica has called it "bananas expensive"—I need to be an actual celebrity, not a celebrity-imitator, to afford it.)

Pregnancy by Jessica, step two: Treat myself. In a 2011 interview with *Lucky* magazine, while pregnant with Haven, Jessica revealed her maternity must-haves. Water, prenatal yoga, and maternity Spanx all made the list, but so did a little TLC. "Pamper yourself, because once the baby comes, you're crazed for a long time. So if you can, indulge, whether it's getting your nails done, or getting a facial, or just spending an extra five minutes to feel pretty in the morning." I appreciate this advice. First of all, it's nice to hear that even Jessica Alba felt a bit frantic after adding to her family. And second of all, yes! Pampering! There are ways to indulge that don't involve French fries, and I need to remember that. Considering I just bought something called mommy-to-be milk bath, I'm ready to dive in.

Step three: Embrace the bump. It's too early for me to have a true pregnant belly, but not too early to consider my new wardrobe. A scroll through Google images shows Jessica's maternity style: She never hides her growing bump, but always looks flawless, whether in a designer dress or a T-shirt and jeans. Per the mom herself, in *Latina* magazine: "If you are sporting a pregnant belly, it's better to show it than to hide it." She gives specific style tips, like opting for V-necks to show off new cleavage (covering it up makes you look fuller on top, she says) and wearing long necklaces that sit atop the belly.

Step four: Accept the flaws. This is going to be the hardest part. The other Alba tips are tangible. I can get into a bubble bath, get out, and check it off the list. But loving my new cellulite? It's not easy. I do want to enjoy pregnancy though, and spending the whole time complaining about my new body might impede that. In a *Self* magazine interview, Jessica didn't exactly praise the changes to her body, but she didn't complain about them, either. "Pregnancy was the most incredible experience that I've ever had. So I'll take the stretch marks. I'll take the sagging boobs. I'll take the cellulite I can never get rid of." They're probably easier to take when you're Jessica Alba, but I can try.

Every day for the next two weeks, after my workout (which is plenty harder when you're growing a person) and shower, I slather myself in organic stretch mark oil and spend an extra five minutes putting on makeup. I stare at my body in shock at how much can change and how quickly—I've already filled out all over—and try to be amused rather than annoyed.

The best thing about having done IVF is that I get an ultrasound nearly every week until the nine-week mark, when I'll be sent back to my OB-GYN. Before today's appointment gets started, Dr. E asks me how I've been feeling.

"Pretty large," I say. "I want to be cute pregnant, not bloated pregnant."

"Yeah, the cute thing doesn't really happen until sixteen weeks," she says. "Until then you'll just feel fat."

My mom might be more excited about this baby than I am. It will be her first grandchild, and when Matt and I broke the news she started crying. Out of happiness. And then, suddenly, out of sadness. My father died six years ago, and it hit her then that he isn't around to see his baby have a baby. Now she's adjusted to the news, and is just annoyed that she's not allowed to tell anybody, since we're waiting to spread the news until I'm further along.

"Rachel, you have a bump!" she says one afternoon.

"I think it's a gut," I say.

"No, that's a pregnant belly." It's too early to be showing for real, but Matt and my mom both agree that I'm looking bigger. Or as my brother so eloquently put it, "You look like you ate a burrito."

* * *

There was a time, not so long ago, when pregnant celebrities were forced to hide their growing bumps and never speak of them. In her book, *A Womb with a View: America's Growing Public Interest in Pregnancy,* author Laura Tropp traces the evolution of pregnancy's role in celebrity culture. "Once, it was forbidden to utter the word 'pregnant' in polite company," she writes. "Even the groundbreaking *I Love Lucy,* which incorporated the star's real life pregnancy, never uttered the word. Now pregnancy is not only popular, but it is also a selling point. Bravo introduced *Pregnant in Heels,* which follows a pregnancy concierge. *Tori & Dean's Inn*

Love gained its popularity, in part, from Tori's very public exposing of her pregnancies throughout the show. . . . Pregnancy is no longer a time to stay out of the limelight but to relish in it."

I was nine years old when a seven-months-pregnant Demi Moore posed nude on the cover of *Vanity Fair*. I still remember that issue sitting on my living room table. The photo has become a pop culture icon and is largely credited with beginning the pregnancy-photo-as-moneymaker craze. In 2005, an American Society of Magazine Editors panel named it the second best magazine cover of the last forty years (the *Rolling Stone* cover of John Lennon and Yoko Ono lying on a bed, him naked in the fetal position, took first place). Today, the Demi photo is one of the most imitated magazine covers of all time—most recently, Jessica Simpson assumed the pose for a 2012 issue of *Elle*.

While the *Vanity Fair* cover was groundbreaking for its time, these days those photos hardly make a stir. We expect pregnant celebrities to show off their bellies, wearing glamorous maternity dresses on the red carpet and $250 maternity jeans on a night out. And if a star doesn't reveal she's expecting, the magazines will speculate anyway, placing any is-she-or-isn't-she star on "bump watch."

As celebrities have embraced baby bumps, their fans have followed suit. Today women flaunt their pregnancies rather than try to cover them up. Bulging bellies are seen as beautiful, even sexy, instead of frumpy and shameful.

There's a downside though. The more we see a pregnant Giselle looking jaw-droppingly gorgeous in a bikini, or pregnant Penelope Cruz flawlessly put together for a date night with Javier Bardem, the more pressure we feel to look glowing and fabulous and perfectly presentable even in the wake of morning sickness, exhaustion, and swelling feet. As Tropp writes, "In the retouched world of celebrity news, pregnant celebs seem to 'do' pregnancy better than anyone else. The glorification of celebrity pregnancy paints a world where celebrities simply revel in their newfound, worry-free motherhood."

Take Tori Spelling's birth scene in *Tori & Dean,* which Tropp calls out. "Just because you're in the hospital and about to have your uterus slashed open, doesn't mean you can't be fashionable," Tori said, in a designer birthing gown, just before a C-section. Or look at Tracy Anderson, the celebrity trainer who caused a stir when she told *DuJour* magazine that "a lot of women use pregnancy as an excuse to let their bodies go, and that's the worst thing. . . . I've seen so many women who come to me right after [having children] with disaster bodies that have gone through hell." The message here is that pregnant or not, we should keep ourselves in pristine condition.

During her pregnancy, Tori Spelling wrote a blog post for the *Today* show claiming pregnant women everywhere should listen to their bodies and "be bump proud." She wrote, "A pregnant woman in any shape or size is beautiful! Pregnancy is an amazing journey and we preggers should be able to show it off. . . . Embrace your curves and bourgeoning belly." But the post was published with a photo of the author in a bikini, looking like a size double zero with her perky cleavage and tiny belly, so it's hard to take her message seriously.

As anyone who has ever read a tabloid knows, the pregnancy headlines don't stop once a celebrity gives birth. Instead, the focus shifts to "body after baby!" And after nine months of dissecting a star's maternity fashions, the eyes of the world turn directly to the offspring and his or her mini-wardrobe. Just look at Suri Cruise, who at four months old was better dressed than I've ever been in my life. Her impeccable style has even inspired blogs like "Suri's Burn Book." (Subtitle: "Just because you don't have a Ferragamo handbag doesn't mean you can behave like a child. [I'm looking at you, Shiloh.]")

All these expectations we have of celebrities—losing the baby weight in weeks, dressing the kids in only the most fashionable clothes—we ultimately expect of ourselves, as well. The standards are impossible to live up to.

Another danger of the whole bump obsession is that it is increasingly easy to mistake a favorite pregnant star for a pregnancy expert. "Information about everything from breast pumps to epidurals was once transmitted locally, from generation to generation, mother to daughter, or friend to friend, but in the 20th century, the source of authority began to shift to popular culture, specifically, to the self-help guru, who offered more than just standard advice on clean towels and hot water," author Daniel Harris wrote on Salon.com in 2006, long before this pregnancy glorification reached its fever pitch. "Now an entirely new mentoring system is emerging, one in which the expert is increasingly the star, who is not only charismatic and glamorous but spectacularly well-informed, a fount of wisdom about the arcana of teething, morning sickness, doulas and postnatal Pilates classes. Christy Turlington insists on the importance of using only organic or environmentally friendly shampoos and lotions on one's infant, while Felicity Huffman kneads the tired muscles of her two young daughters with Burt's Bee apricot massage oil."

Reading this, I can't help but wonder what I'm thinking, blindly following Jessica Alba's pregnancy tips instead of asking my doctor for hers.

Not all celebrities have asked for this kind of attention, of course. Sure, some agree to appear naked on magazine covers, and others sell baby photos for millions of dollars. But I have to imagine there are famous women out there who would rather avoid the extra attention altogether. As Harris wrote, "The cult of the pregnant star represents a deeper penetration of this privacy, which has now escalated from mere surveillance to a psychotic episode of stalking."

After Pink had daughter Willow in 2011, she posted pictures to her personal website, explaining that she hoped it would ease the paparazzi attention. "Due to the unsettling, surprisingly aggressive and unsafe measures that the paparazzi seem to be willing to go to in order to secure that 'first shot' of our daughter—stalking us, chasing us in cars and sitting outside of our home all day and all night, [we] decided that we would release personal photos of our Willow, and donate all of the money to charity."

As consumers of celebrity culture, we devour the images of superstar pregnancies and babies. The standards of perfection prevail even during these sensitive nine months, and no matter how hard we try to keep perspective, these ideals seep in.

I do, truly and honestly, want to have a fabulous pregnancy. I want to feel poised and glamorous even in the midst of what is to come. But do I only feel this way because I've been inundated with pictures of what this time can—nay, *should*—be? If Kristen Bell hadn't been so adorable when she was pregnant, or Jennifer Lopez hadn't been so hot while carrying not one but *two* babies, and they both hadn't made it look so easy, would I still be trying so hard? Or would I, as the classic image goes, be getting fat and eating bonbons? I'm really not sure.

While Jessica Alba is my pregnancy gold standard, it's been eighteen months since she's given birth. For some in-the-moment inspiration—or, on a bad day, self-deprecating comparison—there are a number of stars sharing my baby time line. Penelope Cruz, Fergie, and Jessica Simpson are all due around the same time I am. But the biggest newsmakers in the bump-watch world are Kate Middleton and Kim Kardashian. And these pregnancies aren't only the subjects of tabloids and celebrity rags anymore. I first learned of Kim Kardashian's pregnancy on the *Today* show, not *Access Hollywood*. Other reputable news outlets are having a field day with headlines, pitting the two moms-to-be against each other, as if pregnancy is a competition in itself. "Kim Kardashian v. Kate Middleton: Who Has More Fashion Influence?" asks *Time* magazine. "Battle of the Bumps!" "The Great Pregnancy Smack-Down!" "Baby Kimye vs. The Royal Baby!" I can't help but picture the two of them, impeccably dressed with tiny protruding stomachs, throwing punches as they face off in some sort of hyperfertile Hunger Games.

Tropp says some celebrities use pregnancy as a way to connect to fans—stars go through the same weird body changes and bizarre side effects that any woman might—and while I can't say I relate to either Kim or Kate, I do feel an element of "we're in this together" when reading about their upcoming births.

The rational side of me knows that holding myself to a celebrity standard or comparing myself to the likes of Jessica Alba, Kim Kardashian, or Kate Middleton is unreasonable at best, destructive at worst. Pregnancy is a time to go easy on yourself, and expecting perfection now isn't very forgiving. Kate is a princess for God's sake! My baby will be adorable (let's hope) but it won't be royal. Yet the pop-culture obsessive in me can't help but wish I had their level of glam and continuously wonder what more I could do to get it. Stand up straighter? Tweak my makeup? Wear heels during the day?

It's a real internal conflict: I know I shouldn't liken myself to these all-access, no-budget stars, but I do it anyway. I know I'm holding myself to impossible standards, but I don't stop. I want to be kind to myself during pregnancy and ease up on the pressure, but then I shell out $5 to read about Kate's baby bump in whatever magazine has her splashed on the cover this week.

This isn't just my battle. It seems every woman I know is going through a similar celebrity-driven struggle, if not as blatantly, and not necessarily surrounding pregnancy. I may be well versed in entertainment news and the latest celebrity couples, but no more, I've found, than most of my friends or contemporaries. Each of them has an actress or musician or model that she reveres. The more I tell other twenty-, thirty-, and forty-somethings about my quest, the more nods and resounding yesses I'm met with. "I waited in line for hours to see Bethenny Frankel at Costco," one girl tells me. "If I could be any celebrity, I would die to be her." Another tells me she started taking SoulCycle classes when she saw what it did to Kelly Ripa's body.

Most women are smart enough to know we aren't celebrities. Of course, there are plenty of exceptions—the increasing number of reality TV shows make fame a plausible notion for anyone willing to date a bachelor or run through a giant obstacle course or have plastic surgery on camera. You no longer have to be an actress or a musician to be a celebrity. But even if one isn't a "fame whore," or at all celebrity-obsessed, she probably feels the residual effects of the celebrity machine. When the images and headlines are inescapable, we end up holding ourselves to these standards not to be famous, but to be perfect. And we hardly even realize this.

We need to reframe our thinking. If we could stop comparing

ourselves to our favorite stars as if it's our bodies or theirs, our clothes or theirs, or our relationships or theirs, and instead consider the lifestyles we want (and they have) as lofty goals to strive for, we might be better off. Jennifer's body or Gwyneth's kitchen or Tina's work life—those can't be the standards, but they can be the brass rings. Striving to get closer to the life we deem perfect isn't so unhealthy. It's when we treat these celebrity accomplishments as the yardstick against which we measure our own, as if they are the norm and we are the outliers, that we get into dangerous territory.

Jennifer Garner, Julia Roberts, Jessica Alba—they are the exception. We are the rule.

Clearly I'm still working on many of these issues myself—*I want to be perfect! But I want to be sane!*—and being pregnant seems to bring them to light even more. Maybe it's because I'd like to figure it out before I bring another being into the world. I'm not sure I want my kid to watch me imitating someone else rather than being perfectly pleased with who I am. But I do believe in role models, and perhaps seeing a parent continually strive to be better—or at least a better version of herself—is a good thing.

* * *

I've stayed relatively on track during my Jessica Alba pursuit. My version of pampering myself is usually the allowance of a two-hour nap, a luxury most women don't have. From 3–5 P.M., every day, I can be found passed out on the couch, and I don't think Matt is on board with the new lifestyle.

"What do pregnant women who work in an office do?" he asked me one day when I woke up. I get the sense, though he'd never dare say it, that Matt thinks I'm milking the pregnancy as an excuse to sleep. He is in disbelief that there comes a time in the afternoon when I simply cannot keep my eyes open any longer.

"I think they go to bed at 7 P.M.," I say. "I sleep for two hours in the afternoon but then I stay up until 11. Exhaustion is a normal pregnancy symptom. I'm building an ecosystem in here!"

It could be so much worse, I tell him. I could be puking like the Duchess.

Last week I made my first trip to a popular nearby maternity boutique. I don't need anything just yet, but since I was in the neighborhood I picked up a few basics—black leggings and some solid colored long-sleeved shirts that come in one size only. The best part? Strapping on the fake baby bump to see how everything will fit once I bust out of my current jeans. I can already tell that embracing my new body is going to be hard for me. After years of focusing on what to eat, how to work out, and what I weigh, being okay with what already feels like constant weight gain is tough. I'm growing all over—I might actually be carrying this baby in my butt and thighs—and I want to love it, but it's not easy to retrain the brain. This quest started with the pursuit of the perfect body, and that goal is at odds with the current one: to stay healthy and grow a human. There's a mental shift needed that I haven't quite mastered, namely redefining expectations for myself. Maybe when the baby feels more real—when my belly looks more pregnant than beer gut, or when I feel a kick—it will click. I'll get used to the new me.

Or I won't.

Loving my new, cushier, rounder self is the key to step four, right? Accepting the flaws. It's a learning curve.

———

At ten weeks along, I attend my first prenatal yoga class. I've always planned on doing yoga while pregnant, and that Jessica has listed it as a maternity must-have means it's an official order. "I have a bad back and bad knees and it really prepares your body," she told *Lucky* magazine. "The more limber you are and the stronger you are, the easier your birth. And isn't that what everyone wants?"

Wandering into the small studio I feel a bit out of place. Stomachs are bulging everywhere. While I have an ever-changing midsection, I'm still not showing. I wonder if people think I'm in the wrong class.

The woman next to me makes eye contact and smiles. "How far along are you?" she asks.

"Ten and a half weeks," I say.

This woman looks like she could be my real-life pregnancy muse. At nearly eight months she is all stomach and looks amazing. I refrain from asking if she got her glow from using nontoxic products.

"It's cute that you're here so early in your pregnancy," she says as the teacher starts to quiet the room. I detect some condescension, but just smile and say thanks.

This is my first pregnancy activity. I've never before been in a room reserved exclusively for mothers-to-be. It's pretty weird, as if I've joined some sort of cult.

A studio of Stepford wives, except instead of blond hair and pearls we share baby bumps and black leggings.

Amy, our teacher, asks any student in her first trimester to raise her hand. It's only me. A quiet murmur of giggles resound throughout the room. Not in a mean way, really. It's more like, "Oh, honey, you have no idea what's ahead, you don't need to be here until you have an aching back and wretched constipation."

Amy addresses me directly. "In your first trimester, you really can do just about everything," she says. "But it's such a tenuous time—your baby is like a little seed growing inside you, and you want to nourish the seed to be sure it grows, so it's nice to come to prenatal yoga to start that process." She makes birth sound so organic and lovely that I wonder if she too is a student of Jessica Alba.

Ninety minutes later, as class draws to a close, Amy shares one piece of advice as we sit in child's pose. It's a quote from author Jill Churchill. "There is no way to be a perfect mother, and a million ways to be a good one," she says.

I'm thrown by the motherhood reference. I've gotten as far as thinking of myself as a pregnant person. That alone took some getting used to. I spent the last year so focused on wanting a baby that I nearly forgot I was taking on the daunting task of motherhood. But in almost seven months I'll be someone's parent. It's a huge responsibility, to care for and nurture another person, and the concept still feels foreign. In so many ways, I still feel like a kid myself. I still call my own mother for advice or encouragement or chicken soup when I'm sick. The idea that I will be that person for someone else is scary, yes, but also heartening. I'm ready to love someone that much, to sing her to sleep when she doesn't feel good or cheer for his smallest accomplishment. I haven't given any thought to parenting philosophies or sleep training or any of the heated debates raging on the mommy blogs, but this kid and I will take the ride together.

The quote applies to more than just pregnancy. In my pursuit of a more perfect existence, I've made a lot of changes. Most of which have had a genuinely positive effect. But perfection is elusive, if not altogether impossible. There is probably no way to be perfect, but a million ways to be good.

Compared to where I was when I started, I feel good.

* * *

I'm not the only one who thinks Jessica Alba led a pregnancy worth imitating. The actress's first book, *The Honest Life: Living Naturally and True to You,* is a how-to guide for adopting Jessica's lifestyle. "It's one of the main things I talk about with my friends (both single and with families)—we're all working to make healthier choices without an extreme lifestyle overhaul, and we share tips and strategies. It's the reason I created The Honest Company . . . it's also the reason I wrote this book. Because with the help of friends, family, and experts, I've figured out a few things along the way. I wanted to share *my* version of a healthy natural lifestyle—I call it Honest Living—with you." The book is as explicit a guide-to-life as I could have asked for from any of my celebrity inspirations. It's not just about where to buy nontoxic baby toys or which laundry detergent won't give you a rash. Chapters include favorite salad dressing recipes, instructions for getting the perfect red lip, and a list of Jessica's fashion essentials.

The book is another example of the growing trend of celebrity branding. Like Jake Halpern told me at the beginning of this search, many of the rich and famous, especially the beautiful women with throngs of wannabes, aren't content with being merely an actress, or singer, or model. Or actress-singer-model. They want to represent a lifestyle. They aren't just talent, they're personalities. It started with Gwyneth and Goop. A couple of years later, Heidi Klum launched a lifestyle site in conjunction with AOL. And in the months since I began this quest, more of these brands have popped up. Beyoncé started The Beyhive, a destination for "showing off all the inspiring things I come across every single day." Jennifer Hudson wrote a book to chronicle her weight loss and give tips on emulating her body transformation.

It used to be that you had to be Martha Stewart to be, well, Martha Stewart. Now any celebrity with a glue gun and fashion sense can become a guru. (It's mostly women, but not exclusively. Jay Z has his site Jay Z's Life + Times, which showcases "just a bit of inspiration.")

This shouldn't come as a surprise. Today's type-A woman always feels she should be doing more and doing it better, so why wouldn't type-A celebrities feel the same? Why settle for being a rich famous artist when you can be a rich famous artist *and businesswoman*? Clearly we're buying what they're selling, so why wouldn't they cash in on that?

It's on us. If we don't believe celebrities should double as lifestyle experts then we need to stop reading their newsletters, buying their books, and following their tweets. And since I'm not about to cancel my Goop subscription, I'm willing to take responsibility for my part. If millions of women were dying to know where my favorite pizza came from or how I achieved my curls, I'd give it to them, too.

The Honest Life has an entire chapter on creating an "honest baby." While her company's products focus specifically on parenting needs, here Jessica gives explicit pregnancy advice. There are bits of what I've already read—"pregnancy was the most incredible experience ever . . . so I'll take the stretch marks. I'll take the sagging boobs and the cellulite that's never going away"—and a few new pointers as well. I should point out that in no picture of Jessica, and there are many, do her boobs look low or does her skin look dimply. I'm not saying she's lying, but I'd feel better about my own cellulite if I were given some visual evidence of hers. As far as I can tell, she's a goddess.

The book introduces new additions to my Alba-pregnancy

checklist: cure cravings, eat mindfully, exercise, create a birth plan, and find support. Not exactly revolutionary, but sound advice from what I can tell. Exercise I've got down. Support I've got, too. Matt's been great (he lets me play the pregnancy card plenty, catering to my requests for a foot rub without any pushback), my mom lives around the corner and can't wait to babysit, and a handful of pregnant friends have been great about answering questions. Jessica's support system looks different, and apparently consists of her chiropractor, yoga teacher, and a hypnobirthing guide.

That's right, hypnobirthing. The practice, she says, is "where you learn to relax through guided meditation." That sounds reasonable, but the name has me questioning her very simplified explanation. It sounds more like the kind of thing where you get sleepy, very sleepy, and then you come to and there's a baby in your arms and you don't know where the last five hours went. During an appearance on *Ellen,* while pregnant with Haven, Jessica explained the method. "Basically my husband takes me through sort of a meditation. So he's like saying, 'you're relaxed and you're floating on clouds' while you're going through labor and your contractions. . . . I'm just concentrating on breathing and staying relaxed because it's when you get tense that makes the whole labor worse and more painful. That's all it is. It's not like a weird thing."

It sounds pretty weird. I've never been through labor, but I'm pretty sure I won't liken it to floating on clouds. And I'm certain that if Matt tries to act as if I'm floating on a cloud while I push six to nine pounds of human being out of me, I'll punch him in the face.

And yet here I am, on the hypnobirthing website.

According to the official description, hypnobirthing is a

"unique method of relaxed, natural childbirth education enhanced by self-hypnosis techniques." It goes on to list some hypnobirthing statistics: "9.5 percent of hynobirthing mothers chose to birth in the comfort of their home. The national average is less than 1 percent. 6 percent of hypnobirthing mothers chose to birth in freestanding birth centers. The national average is less than 1 percent. Only 23 percent of hypnobirthing mothers birthing vaginally had epidural anesthesia, compared to the national average of 71 percent." These figures don't sell me. Call me unenlightened, but I'm very much looking forward to giving birth in a hospital, surrounded by doctors. And drugs.

To really get a sense of what I'm working with, I go to the world's most dangerous place. YouTube. Plenty of couples have chosen to share their hypnobirthing videos with the world, and I am enough of a glutton for punishment to watch one of them. Big mistake. Not because hypnobirthing is especially hard to watch—from what I can tell the husband is simply whispering meditations into his wife's ear—but now that there's a baby inside me, there's no reason to witness someone else give birth. I've only ever seen the pretty, glossed over, Hollywood version of labor. This video isn't graphic or anything—I see no birth canals or baby body parts—but this woman does not look comfortable. Despite the video's subtitles ("Still calm!") she seems pretty miserable. There are quick yelps of pain that make me wince as I watch. And then suddenly she's on the birthing table on all fours, like a cow.

I do not need to see this.

I can only find two hypnobirthing classes in the Chicago area, and they both cost $350 for four three-hour sessions. At nearly $30 an hour, they're pricey. They're also both an hour away.

When I picture being in this class with Matt for three hours at a time, I get preemptively embarrassed. Matt does yoga. He believes in my new adoption of personal meditation. But as a couple, we're not the guided meditation type. I don't think we could take each other seriously during a potential flight through the clouds.

Still, if he's game I am.

I shoot him a text. "Want to take a hypnobirthing class? Jessica Alba does it. You could guide me through meditation to make birthing easier. $350."

I'm at home while he's running errands, and an hour later I haven't heard back. I text again. "Is that a no?"

Five minutes later my phone rings. "What is this exactly?" Matt asks.

"It's supposed to ease labor," I say. "You'll guide me through meditations, and I'll feel like I'm floating on a cloud."

Matt doesn't shoot me down entirely. "If you want to do it because you think it will help, okay," he says. "If you want to do it because Jessica Alba does it, no."

The man has a point. This is where the whole celebrity-as-expert issue comes into play. I have to choose where to draw the line. Jessica has given birth twice, sure, but so have billions of other women. Neither my reproductive endocrinologist nor my doctor have mentioned hypnobirthing. That doesn't make it bad—it obviously works wonders for some people—but it also reminds me that it's far from necessary.

To be fair, Jessica Alba doesn't purport to be a birthing expert. She calls in some experts throughout her book's pregnancy chapter and clarifies that "I'm sharing what worked for me, but that doesn't mean you need to do the same—every family's needs are different and special."

Still, it's easy to mistake someone who has a book on parenting for an authority on parenting.

Matt's point is an important one. Do I think hypnobirthing will help me? Or am I suggesting it only because Jessica Alba does it? Considering my "birth plan" is simply to bring a healthy baby into the world, using whatever means necessary, the cloud-floating probably isn't for me.

We decide to keep our $350. Might as well start saving for this kid's college now.

If I have one complaint about Jessica's guidance, it has nothing to do with hypno anything. It's the section on curing your cravings. It should be my favorite piece of advice, and it would be, except it seems that my body and Jessica's want different things. Her cravings were for watermelon and citrus fruit. Mine are for Hershey's Kisses. "The best way to deal with cravings?" she asks. "Go eat whatever it is your body says it needs, especially if it's fresh and healthy. . . . Don't question the logic. Your body knows what it's doing."

During a coffee date with a pregnant friend, I share this bit of advice. "Jessica Alba writes in her book that we should indulge our pregnancy cravings," I say. "But then she says she only craved fresh fruits and veggies."

"I listened to my pregnancy cravings on Friday," my friend tells me. "I went to the McDonald's drive-through and pulled over down the street from work to eat in hiding like I was the star of an A&E special."

Been there.

I don't think there's a pregnant woman in America who is struggling with whether to indulge her craving for a celery stick or an apple. If you want salad you should eat it? Thanks for the tip. My cravings come in the sugar variety, which apparently don't fall in that same eat-what-you-want category. "If you're craving superprocessed foods, talk to your OB-GYN or midwife about your diet because you might be lacking nutrients," Jessica says.

These celebs are my imaginary best friends until they say something that makes me roll my eyes. Then I join the army of cynics.

No wonder fame is so fleeting.

It's not easy living a nontoxic existence. A person would need to study for years, not a month, before getting a feel for it. *The Honest Life* has a helpful index, with a list of "dishonest ingredients" to look out for, but the list spans five pages and some of the ingredients are umbrella terms, and what is listed on the actual packaging of your shampoo or nail polish might be totally different. After ten minutes of studying the hand soap and air freshener in my apartment, I find that the air freshener definitely contains a dishonest ingredient (propylene glycol) and the soap contains at least one (fragrance) but probably more like five. The packaging mentions that the product is cruelty-free, not tested on animals, and biodegradable, which originally tricked me into thinking it was nontoxic—a common mistake, says Jessica. Figuring all this out takes ten minutes for only two products. At this rate, a trip to the drugstore will take three hours.

Now that I know how much I don't know, I only trust products made entirely of hemp.

* * *

My mother, who, like Jessica, had two children, is getting sick of my panicked phone calls. "Nothing is happening," I tell her one day. "I'm not sick, I don't feel anything going on in there. I think there's something wrong with the baby."

A few days later I have a new concern. "I'm eating too much sugar. Do you think I have gestational diabetes?"

And some days after that. "The baby looked weird on the ultrasound. Not the way the others on the Internet look. I hope there isn't anything wrong with it."

My mother's loving response: "You need a tranquilizer."

To hear Jessica tell it, pregnancy should be tranquilizer enough. "Being pregnant is kind of like a sedative," she told E! back when she was carrying Honor. "Everything is chill and I don't get as anxious about things. . . . If I freak out, it affects the baby. I'm trying to stay chill."

It's a different story than the one she tells in her book, where she writes that she was "pretty much in panic mode" during her first pregnancy. But I'd like to get to that chill place.

The next time I decide that my pregnancy has gone south just because I didn't nap that day, I'll take a breath.

Chilling out, though harder than it looks, might even be the key to the whole you've-got-it-together vibe. Nobody ever looked glamorous while having a panic attack.

* * *

As I suspected, pregnancy and perfection don't go hand in hand. Three months in, I'm so happy to be carrying a little one that I'm willing to sacrifice a little glamour if need be. But since getting my quest back on track, I must admit I feel better. Working out, eating (relatively) healthier, meditating, getting back to work—it's all making a difference. I'm pampering myself, dressing my growing bump, embracing my cravings (still Hershey's Kisses), and sometimes denying them ("eat mindfully"). I'm doing my best to embrace my flaws and live as nontoxic a life as I can.

I'm not hypnobirthing and I'm okay with that.

In interviews, Jessica Alba mentions perfection often. Her definition of the word has evolved, she says. "Now that I've had two kids, my idea of physical perfection has changed," she told *Women's Health*. "I finally feel confident, secure, and, yes, sexy." And her expectations of herself have shifted. "There's no such thing as perfect and you can't possibly do everything all the time and that's okay. I always had this idea of perfection and wanting to be the best mom, the best wife, the best daughter, the best sister or the best friend and the best at my acting," she told *People*. "You cannot be pulled in those different directions. I wish someone would have told me that earlier. It would've relieved so much stress."

I have to say I'm grateful to Jessica for this one. Not for saying there's no such thing as perfect—every celebrity knows to say that while still seeming perfectly perfect—but for admitting that she was, at least once upon a time, as obsessed with perfection as the rest of us. It's like when Julianne Moore admitted to Yahoo! that "I hate dieting. I hate having to do it to be the 'right size.' I'm hungry all the time." The occasional reminder that celebrities put as much pressure on themselves as we regular women do, that it's not all effortless and they don't all roll out of bed as glamorous as they appear, that's the greatest kindness they can give us. Because sometimes it's not the need to seem flawless that gets us down, but the fact that it seems to come so easily to everyone else.

CHAPTER EIGHT

BEYONCÉ: THE WHOLE PACKAGE

"I'm a perfectionist."
—NFL Network press conference

"I'm still trying to learn that I don't have to kill myself and be so hard on myself and be so critical and I can smell the roses. I don't want to never be satisfied. I don't think that's a healthy way to live."
—Life Is But a Dream, HBO

"I didn't feel that I looked beautiful during birth, but who does? After being pumped with all those fluids and gaining so much weight ... I barely recognized myself."
—People

It's been seven months since starting this quest, and I've upgraded every area of my life and even added a new wrinkle with the pregnancy. I've taken the celebrities that have so often made me feel inadequate and done my best to turn them into role models to strive toward rather than standards to which I compare myself. Everyone has her own version of perfect, and I've figured out mine. I know what the ideal, most-fabulous-version-of-me day looks like, even if I'm not always successful at practicing it.

One of the lessons I've learned over the past months is that achieving my goals isn't impossible. Maybe sheer perfection isn't realistic, but I can set specific intentions and do the work to realize them. If I want to badly enough, there are ways to lose weight and get that hot body, or master the kitchen, or dress with a signature style. Even if I'm on a budget and even if I'm short on time. After all, I didn't find the secret to happiness in a Gwyneth cleanse, and I didn't spend $500 on a personal trainer or a magic face cream. My most satisfying achievements were the simpler changes—the ten minutes of meditation or the fifteen minutes in front of the Tracy Anderson exercise videos. Time and money are a luxury for sure—and the fact that celebrities have more of both certainly makes the glamorous life more accessible—but the real question that determines whether we become our so-called perfect selves is nothing more than this: How much do we want it? If we crave something badly enough, we make it a priority. If we crave something in theory, but not enough to work for it, we probably won't get it.

I know this to be true for myself. When I started out this quest, I wanted Jennifer Aniston's body. Spoiler alert! I still don't look like Jen. And not because I'm pregnant. I didn't look like Jen three months ago, either. But I do work out five days a week now, which is a huge change from the twice-a-week-on-a-good-week I had whittled down to when I was feeling my most blechy. The change that didn't really take: the eating. To say I eat salmon and kale every day would be a lie. I'd like it to be true, but the idea of actually living off those superhealthy, semitasteless foods makes me want to crawl into a hole. Completely transforming my body isn't worth that to me. (Not to mention the fact that since getting pregnant, I have a severe fish aversion.) I stick with the workouts because they make me feel healthy and strong and like it's okay when I eat a little more so-called shit than I should.

In her HBO documentary *Life Is But a Dream*, Beyoncé talks at length about firing her father as her manager. At one point she tells the camera, "The first decision I had to make as my manager was 'What do you want?'" Did she want to be successful on the radio? On tour? Or did she want to focus on her personal life? It's a simple, but powerful, question.

When I started on this journey, I too tried to figure out what I wanted. The answer: to be perfect. The closer I came, the happier I would be. Or such was my reasoning. The rational side of me knew there was no such thing as perfection, but I wanted to feel the way I imagined those celebrities in the tabloids did. Fabulous. Confident. Together. Happy.

I know now that perfection isn't an answer to the "what do I want?" question. The answer should be tangible. I want to lose weight. I want to dress better. I want to feel more calm.

Had I seen this more clearly seven months ago, my answer would have been twofold: 1) I want to go to sleep at night feeling good about what I accomplished that day, and 2) I want to have a baby. If any two desires have driven my actions over the course of this quest, it's those.

In an interview with *Self*, Beyoncé spoke about her—I'll say it—perfect body. "The truth is, it's a lot of sacrifice," she said. "It's more about your mental strength than physical strength. You have to push yourself. It doesn't matter what trainer you have. And it doesn't matter what program you're on. You have to be healthy and make choices." From what I've learned, that applies to so much more than the physical self.

I came to these realizations after looking at what I tried to accomplish, and what I actually did accomplish. I'm someone who is pretty good at setting a goal and following through, especially when the game plan has structure, like "identify what your favorite celebrities do, then do the same." That's a fairly clear directive, and once the specific to-do list has been identified, the follow-through shouldn't be so hard. But some of the things I identified (the salmon and kale, the hypnobirthing, the cleanse) just didn't feel worth it. In the end, I knew they wouldn't make me especially happy or fulfilled. (Salmon and kale sometimes: yes. Always: no.)

For me, fitting in a tough workout, putting on an outfit that makes me feel confident and presentable, logging productive work hours, eating relatively healthy, and spending quality time with Matt or some friends, those things alone make me feel good at the end of the day. Now that I'm pregnant, I can add personal pampering to that list. (Since I'm further along now, my pampering usually takes the form of a long shower, a slathering of baby lotion, or a thirty-minute nap. The excessive sleeping has subsided, thankfully.) On the days when I cook a Gwyneth recipe and meditate for twenty full minutes and eat only the superfoods? Then I've killed it. But that doesn't happen all that often.

It should go without saying that everyone's near-perfect day looks different. When I told a friend that I was doing this quest, she told me, "I could not care less about working out. I hate it. I have no desire to do it. But I would give my left arm to be more Gwynethy in the kitchen." So I say, pick a lane. Or two. Your perfect day and my perfect day will look very different, but if we're both walking around feeling accomplished and confident at the end of it, we've both won.

Perhaps this sounds like I've come to some wise conclusions that have made me totally happy and at peace with my life.

Not entirely. There's a difference between knowing something intellectually and actually living it day to day. I've gained some self-acceptance through this journey, but I still wish I could do more. I still want to do it all, in fact, and then some—I wish my closet were more organized and my makeup were more creative and that I walked around with the glow of the most confident and fabulous celebrity. I still click through pictures of stars online wishing I had a little more of this and a little less of that. The pangs of "if only I could be like her" are still there, if less acute. The difference now is that I try to use that as the root of inspiration rather than frustration.

I've also learned that many of those feelings of inadequacy are manufactured and perpetuated by the magazines or websites or TV shows that feed us our celebrity news. They use headlines and photo layouts to make us feel like we should want to be like these celebs—and that we *almost* can be—so that we keep buying more product.

We want to be like Jennifer Aniston, or Gwyneth Paltrow, or Sarah Jessica Parker, or whomever because we think they've got it all. They are beautiful, successful, well dressed. Perfect.

But are these people even happy? I certainly don't know, and unless you're an Aniston or your best friend is a Paltrow, you don't, either. So in the end, this quest hasn't even been about the actual celebrities. It's about our perception of them. When I spoke to Jake Halpern, author of *Fame Junkies,* he told me a story I'll never forget. "I was in India last year working on an article, and I went into the house of a guy living in the slums, and on the wall he had pictures of Jesus, Buddha, Krishna, Mother Teresa, and Arnold Schwarzenegger," he told me. "I said, 'Arnold? Why?' And he said, 'All the people on this wall have some important meaning to me. They represent some attribute that I aspire to, whether it is generosity or peace. Schwarzenegger, for me, represents self-improvement and making yourself out of nothing and living a healthy lifestyle and keeping your body healthy.' When he said it, it didn't seem as crazy as it did initially. This image of Schwarzenegger was as important to him as these other gods. It doesn't make a difference what that picture means to me. It's what he drew from it. I look at it and think *Total Recall* or *Commando,* but he looks at that picture and it represents something powerful and redeeming."

High-minded journalists and media critics love to hate on our celebrity culture and belittle anyone who buys into it. They'll tell you it's a story with no good guy. The celebrities are bad for catering to the hype and dismissing their carefully groomed images as "just me being myself." The media is evil for stalking these celebrities and creating narratives that feed the frenzy, and for making us regular folk feel like we could be just like them—if only we buy this one issue. And women like me, who admit to being interested in—and influenced by—celebrity culture are silly, unintelligent, even pathetic.

After all this time, I know it's not so simple. Some people—me, for example, or that man in the Indian slums—enjoy having role models, and do well by it. I've always paid attention to others and studied their success to see what I could glean from their lives. It's not limited to celebrities—I read memoirs and blog posts from writers I admire, or profiles of dancers who fascinate me. But we choose the models we look up to from those in front of us. It's the rare person who says "I need a muse, let me go find her." So it's no wonder that women—smart, self-respecting, strong women—might have a celebrity or two they can't get enough of. One can have different role models in different areas. Not each of them has to be a Nobel prize winner. They can be an athlete, or an actress, or a mogul, or a fashionista. We shouldn't be faulted for who we admire.

Celebrity culture isn't going anywhere. Stars will continue to be a part of our inner lives. We'll continue to make lists of dream dinner guests and "freebies," those rankings of the celebrities we're allowed to sleep with, free of repercussions from our real-life partners, should the occasion arise. And as celebrity reality shows become increasingly popular, and more stars sign on to Twitter, we'll feel an even deeper connection to our favorite famous faces.

The danger comes when we forget that the story we're being sold isn't the whole truth. A celebrity can post as many selfies as she wants, but she usually isn't posting the one of her cellulite and bad skin. As long as I remember that what I perceive to be perfect isn't necessarily so, and as long as I can strive for perfection while still forgiving myself when I fall short, I'm safe.

* * *

I'm nearing the end of this experiment in self-improvement, but I have no intention of going back to my old ways. Sitting around in pajamas all day, passing on exercise in favor of sleep, and working just enough to get by didn't suit me. I was sluggish and frustrated and frazzled. In another six months, that kind of life won't be an option anyway. I'm pretty sure babies don't have a snooze button and I'll need whatever serenity I can muster just to maintain my sanity.

So now's the time to put it all together. Each month I've tried to build on the month before, but this month is for extra credit. Can I, for just a little while, do it all? And do it all well? And if I can, will I give off that glow of the rich and famous? Or at least the poised and confident?

There is no one who represents the peak of perfection like Beyoncé Knowles. Or is it Carter-Knowles? Or Knowles-Carter? It hardly matters, as B has achieved one-name status.

Beyoncé is everywhere. At the Super Bowl, at President Obama's inauguration, on magazine covers ("The Sexiest Woman of the Century" according to *GQ*, the face of *Vogue*'s annual Power Issue) and TV (her self-produced, self-directed documentary, for example). I watched her Super Bowl performance with two other women and we all stared at the screen with our jaws on the floor. "She's so hot," one said. "She looks insane," said another. ("Insane" being a term of the highest praise.) And then me: "I want to be her when I grow up. I mean, look at her."

The men in the group were almost more mesmerized by our Beyoncé worship than by Beyoncé herself. Almost.

She really does seem to have it all: the body, the talent, the marriage, the kid, the confidence, the serenity. If I didn't love her so much, I'd hate her.

In all my research, I did find one flaw, if you can even call it that. Beyoncé can't cook. Or so she says. But this is comforting for all of thirty seconds, until I remember that she's best friends with Gwyneth, so she can get her home-cooked meals from her pal.

I said there's no such thing as true perfection, but I take it back. It is Beyoncé.

This image comes at a cost with fans, though. Beyoncé is not relatable. She doesn't have the girl-next-door quality of the Jennifers, she isn't a celebrity you think you could be best friends with, and her level of excellence doesn't feel attainable. She is the "World's Most Beautiful Woman," according to *People*. Queen B, who "runs the world," per *Vogue*. "Imminent World Domination" warns Jezebel.com. Even *The New York Times* called Beyoncé "the woman with everything."

In a review of Beyoncé's documentary for *New York* magazine, pop critic Nitsuh Abebe writes, "Not a thing about [*Life Is But a Dream*] . . . runs any risk of rejecting the over-the-top hero worship that's accumulated around [Beyoncé], or her status as an impossible yardstick of fulfillment and achievement. It is, perhaps, bad news for the friend who recently told my wife she found that Super Bowl show a little depressing: 'You feel like you've got it together, and then you look at *her*.'"

It's true. After a day of researching Bey—watching interviews and movies, reading magazine articles, all of it—I feel like an underachiever, but I'm also inspired. Watching her performances on the HBO documentary, I want to get up and dance. In fact, I do just that. But first I download two more of her songs, "Love on Top" and "Run the World (Girls)." Which means whatever she's doing she's doing right, because I just spent the last five hours researching the Queen B, only to give her more of my money.

Here's what I've learned: Beyoncé is a perfectionist. The theme of control—over her performances, her image, her branding—comes up again and again. There's her Tumblr blog, iam.beyonce.com, a collection of meticulously curated photos of the star and her loved ones—Jay Z, Blue Ivy, President Obama—that will steal hours of your life. "This is my life, today, over the years—through my eyes," she writes. "My family, my travels, my love. This is where I share with you, this will continue to grow as I do."

The photos are billed as candid and personal, but I don't believe for a second that a picture of Jay Z pushing his wife on a swing in the middle of a giant field was taken on just another afternoon. And I'm someone who wants to buy the images celebrities are selling. B is clearly picking the persona she wants to present on this blog, and I doubt there's a candid, off-the-cuff shot in the bunch. As *GQ* writer Amy Wallace points out, "It stands to reason that when a girl owns her every likeness, as Beyoncé does, it can make her even more determined to be perfect. (Beyoncé isn't just selling Beyoncé's music, of course; she's selling her iconic stature:

a careful melding of the aspirational and the unattainable.)" And there's her own admission that she is nearly impossible to please. "I'm still trying to learn that I don't have to kill myself and be so hard on myself and be so critical and I can smell the roses," she says in *Life Is But a Dream*. "I don't want to never be satisfied. I don't think that's a healthy way to live."

This story of Beyoncé the perfectionist is the theme of so many profiles. More so than her talent or her voice, journalists talk about her façade. They say her image is so carefully crafted that it's nearly impossible to know the person behind the persona. "We may not actually know much about Beyoncé," Nitsuh Abebe writes, "but there is a model of perfection we would like to see in her, and the fact that she can sustain that image suggests she has it really, really, *rigorously* together."

Beyoncé would have fans believe that she's just like us, struggling to be the best version of herself while trying to let go of her control issues. "Stop pretending that I have it all together," she tells herself on camera. But few critics buy into this. "*Life Is But a Dream* is nothing but an exercise in public togetherness; even the webcam confessionals and a tender speech about her miscarriage can't hide the obvious calculation behind the self-directed film," writes *Vulture* journalist Amanda Dobbins. "You can take that as a stab at self-improvement, or you can take it as a savvy attempt to answer her critics in the middle of a film designed to reinforce her Perfect image."

So either B is just like us, or she wants to appear just like us to further her own empire.

The refreshing news, for those of us who think we should be waking up more perfect every day, is that it clearly takes exorbitant amounts of work to be Beyoncé. Take this typical day from 2009, documented in *Vogue* before she even had a baby: "She got up at the crack of dawn in the Tribeca loft she shares with Jay Z . . . , ate a tiny portion of Honey Nut Cheerios, ran six miles, and then worked out with her trainer, who had her in every imaginable kind of squat to get her ready to fit into her no doubt skintight Theirry Mugler–designed tour costumes. Then she went to a dance rehearsal for a couple of hours before showing up here. Now she will sit for a meeting with her management, scarf down several bites of a salad with jalapeños and avocado ('so that it tastes like something that's bad for you'), do this interview, and then rejoin the dance rehearsal until late into the night. 'And then I have to go home and be a wife!' she says, laughing."

There's no reason to feel bad for her, but it's good to be reminded that the fabulousness takes more effort than *Us Weekly* would have us believe.

Though my ultimate fantasy is to live a life that includes hours of dance rehearsal (I'm still hoping to put that tutu to its intended use), I can't copy this sample day. Perhaps because I have no management, and no trainer, and no one begging to interview me. Studying Beyoncé has made me aspire to supposed perfection both more and less. I'm conflicted, as usual, between "look what I could achieve if I wanted it as badly as she does" and "that kind of self-imposed pressure sounds unbearable." But beyond the constant documentation of Beyoncé's perfectionism, I do cull some specific insights that help round out my daily to-dos.

On exercise: "I'll put on a song that I really like and do biceps curls with five-pound weights for the whole song and just try to burn it out."

My Aniston-level cardio classes are going to ease up eventually, given the baby and all, and I happen to have a set of three-pound weights at home, so this sounds like a good plan. I can certainly pound out some biceps curls to one of my favorite Beyoncé tracks, "Ring the Alarm," and I can even dance around the house to "Single Ladies" for a little heart rate action.

On food: "I'm not trying to lose or gain weight, but I do have to work out and watch what I eat. I'm not someone who can go crazy. I'll usually have cereal for breakfast and a salad for lunch and a light dinner, and then on Sundays I'll allow myself to have whatever I want."

That diet plan is from her pre-pregnancy days. When she had to lose the baby weight—she's admitted to gaining fifty-seven pounds with Blue—B has said that she steered clear of "anything delicious" and had zero cheat days. But since I won't be gearing up for a Super Bowl performance or a world tour, I'll embrace her mandate of Sunday cheat days when trying to lose my own baby weight. Even her pre-pregnancy eating plan will serve me well.

On fashion: "Every day in my life is a part of my history, and I've worked really hard on my career and my life. So I make sure I wouldn't be upset if somebody saw me. I've been mostly wearing my hair slicked back in a ponytail and no makeup, just sunglasses and lip gloss."

This is a surprisingly helpful reminder, and a great addendum to my SJP-inspired style guidelines. Wear a good shoe and great purse, don't be swayed by trends, know your figure, own a statement piece—these are all great rules. But on the days when it's snowing out and I'm feeling more fat than pregnant and also a little nauseous, I have broken them in favor of sweats and a T-shirt. It goes against everything I learned—dress better to feel better!—but it happens. And then I take a quick walk to the 7-11, wearing a sweatshirt from high school and dirty pants, and inevitably run into someone I know. That I never see anyone familiar when I've done my makeup or forced myself into a cute pair of jeans is just one of the world's cruel jokes. But what of this middle ground that Beyoncé mentions? Make sure I wouldn't be upset if somebody saw me. That, if anything, is a foolproof fashion guideline. I wouldn't mind if someone saw me in comfy leggings and a cute T-shirt, and my hair in a wispy bun. It's easier than getting dolled up, but still more attractive than sweatpants with holes.

Also, sunglasses and lip gloss. Yes.

On work ethic: "I still have to work on my time management, because I have great opportunities and it's really hard saying no."

For much of my life I've advocated saying yes to everything. It's a mantra that has come in handy both personally and professionally, but the idea that I can and should say no every now and then is powerful. I love seeking out and taking on new projects, but there's such a thing as being overextended.

On marriage: "Never be predictable. Mix it up, surprise him, change your hair—be the woman he knows with a little bit of a twist."

After six years of staying mum on her relationship with Jay Z, Beyoncé has opened up recently. Mostly it's the typical wisdom about respect and friendship and sacrifice, but this "be the woman with a twist" advice intrigues me. Change it up? I am a fairly predictable wife. I haven't changed my hair in, approximately, ever. I can't imagine how Matt must feel about the fact that by the time he gets home from work most nights, I've already changed into my comfy clothes, even on the days I go the extra mile to look cute. When I think to myself, "nobody will see me, who cares what I look like?" it's as if I've completely forgotten that Matt is somebody, and perhaps the person I should want to look good for more than anyone. I love that he loves me even in my least adorable outfits, but maybe I should pay some heed to this "woman with a twist" advice. A little extra effort shows a level of care that would be nice to communicate.

On serenity: "Anyone can plan a staycation, just make the decision to take time for yourself and explore. Eat alone at your favorite restaurant or the one you've always wanted to try. Go to a day spa instead of getting the quick mani-pedi. Grab a friend and visit the closest winery. I'm grateful for the time I gave myself to breathe, to relax, and to be inspired. My personal retreat gave me strength and a creative reawakening. I returned refreshed, renewed, and empowered to reevaluate my life and do things that will make a difference."

Of all the Beyoncé-isms, this might be the most out of touch with her fans, as few women can take a staycation at a day spa or a winery. But most can at least take a momentary break and escape to a restaurant for a meal or a museum for an afternoon. Sometimes the best way to clear your head is to get out of your head.

On pregnancy: "The baby is coming in three weeks. I feel anxious. These last three weeks are my last three weeks responsible for myself, so I'm trying my best to take care of my childlike self and enjoy my freedom."

This is a great reminder for me. I've been so excited about the upcoming baby, and so wrapped up in pregnancy, that I haven't thought much about the fact that in six months, I'll never be just me anymore. There will always be someone I feel responsible for and linked to in a way I'm pretty sure I can't yet comprehend. And so I need to take time to be a kid. I need to sleep way too late on a Saturday morning and stay up long past my bedtime on a Saturday night. I should spend a day watching rom-coms on the couch. Or going to movies. Or reading books. Before we started trying, whenever Matt and I spent a Sunday morning reading the paper and watching a TBS movie marathon, he would remind me that this was why we weren't ready for kids. "Once there are children, we'll never do this again," he'd say. I don't believe life is over once you start a family, but I'm sure it will be harder to act like a child when I'm also responsible for one.

I remember being 15 and lying around the house complaining that I was "soooo boooooorrred." I need to spend some time being bored. Boredom will most definitely be a luxury in the not-too-distant future.

That Beyoncé has been quoted regarding every single aspect of my perfect lifestyle—from the clothes to the work to the serenity to the pregnancy—speaks to her status as the whole package. Outlets as varied as *The Atlantic* and *Us Weekly*, *NPR* and *TMZ*, hail her as the woman who has it all.

Most of the celebrity muses I've adopted over this journey have been in their forties. Jennifer, Gwyneth, Sarah Jessica, Tina, Jennifer, Julia. I've found solace in our ten-year difference. It was reassurance that maybe this whole endeavor is a testament to my youth, and I'll get wiser, more content, and more confident in a decade or so.

Beyoncé is eight months older than me, almost to the day (she, 9/4/81; me 5/5/82). That she has taken over the world at 31 makes her even more aspirational. There is no fooling myself into thinking I can be like B. But that doesn't make the goal any less worth pursuing. I won't be following myself with a video diary or dodging paparazzi, but if I can feel that level of confidence—dare I say ferocity?—in my own life, even for a day, it might be the high I need.

To cap off this journey, it's time to do it all. It's not about homing my focus in on one aspect anymore. Now I need to integrate all of these lessons into one livable life. While I'm happy to have role models, and it's great to find inspiration in others, I need to find my own version of perfect without consulting *People*. I need to know if doing it all will be enough. I'm trying for one perfect day. If I hit my every mark, will I go to bed feeling fabulous and accomplished and proud and confident? Or will I always feel like there is more to be done, that I'm still not enough?

I've stopped even trying to wake up early—call it embracing my childlike self—so instead I get up at 8 A.M. with my alarm, thirty minutes before my workout class is to start. After an hour of running and weight lifting, I pick up a fruit-and-veggie smoothie for breakfast. It's filled with strawberries, blueberries, kale, spinach, beets, and broccoli and seems pretty similar to the offerings in Jennifer Aniston's chefs' cookbook. On the walk home, it occurs to me that if I really wanted to do it right I'd be making this drink at home instead of buying it at Jamba Juice. I can almost hear Gwyneth admonishing me in my ear: "All that sugar!" Which means I've been awake for less than two hours and I've already had my first "I should have done more" moment.

After a quick shower, I spend a little extra time applying my all-natural, nontoxic, organic body cream—made with cocoa butter and sea buckthorn extract (I have no idea what sea buckthorn is, but it certainly sounds earthy)—to fulfill Jessica's mandate that I pamper myself. My Dove deodorant is probably toxic and not

Jessica-approved, but I apply it anyway, because it's that or body odor.

I spend more time, still, getting dressed. When your office is your living room, you'd think choosing an outfit would be a fairly mindless endeavor. But I've got my growing belly to consider (fourteen weeks!) and many of the clothes that were once cute are now snug. I want an outfit that makes me feel confident in, rather than embarrassed by, my new belly. I need to feel presentable—both so I won't mind running into someone I know, and so that I'll have that extra enclothed cognition push. If I'm dressed like a slob, I'll work like a slob. (Dressing like a writer is a tricky mandate since we're not known for much more than pajama pants.) I opt for a pair of jeans and a white button-down blouse. Something about a crisp white shirt reminds me of Diane Sawyer, and I figure she's been pretty productive with her life.

I sit down at the computer with my water bottle next to me. (Water! Celebrities love water! Skin, energy, immune system—it's the miracle drug! Plus, since getting pregnant, Matt's been on me about hydration. Out with the soda, in with the H_2O.) The plan is to write one thousand words before lunch, enough to make a significant dent in my workload. Other office busywork will come later, but this is my time to tap into my creativity and do the work that made me want to be a writer. Five pages—or a thousand words—can go fairly quickly if you're in the zone.

Done. Channeling Tina on the work ethic, combined with Julia on the "no social media," makes for a productive morning. I've even run two loads of laundry—productivity begets productivity, I guess.

Lunch is tricky. If this really is going to be the perfect day, I should probably be making Gwyneth's Ivy Chopped Salad. But if

I want to be the butt-kicking worker that is Tina or Beyoncé, I can't take another hour or two to whip up a restaurant-style salad. I err on the side of Tina and order a salad from a restaurant down the street. The plus side? I don't stare at the ground while I'm walking to pick it up so as not to make eye contact with any familiar faces. I've got makeup on, I look winter chic in my snowboots, and I'm ready to bump into someone. Anyone.

Which of course means there's no one in sight.

After lunch I grab a pillow and head to the bathroom. It's still my meditation room, and I use the pillow to sit on. Today's goal is to finally go the entire twenty minutes without glancing at the timer. I always convince myself I must have missed the gong, but no, it's just that it's hard to be still for so long. It's a struggle to keep my mind from wandering, it's difficult to sit up straight, and it's tough on my hips—especially with a growing uterus bearing down on my joints.

Fifteen minutes in, I cave and look at the timer. I can't stop myself. Meditation will never come naturally to me. I get fidgety, and the more I wonder if the time is almost up, the more I feel my heart pounding in my chest. I have not experienced that moment of enlightenment where I leave my own body and watch my meditating self from above. But the timer still says, "Relax. Focus on your breathing," so I try to do just that. Despite my poor meditation skills, I'd like to stick with it over the coming months. The scientifically proven benefits—one study found that those who meditated for thirty minutes a day for eight weeks improved their memory, sense of self, empathy, and stress—are even more convincing than the whole Julia Roberts in Taos bit.

Post-meditation, it's back to work. Writing, emails, the usual.

When Matt gets home at 5:30, I follow him around the apartment like a puppy. After a day with no social interaction, I crave human contact. This is why I work at the local coffee shop most days, but since today was spent squarely in my own living room I try to get my social fill from my husband. I also need to steal moments with him when I can. Jennifer Garner says so, and thus it must be true. He's heading out in a minute to play basketball— "don't wait for me to eat," he says—so we have the usual chatter. His day, my day, how my growing belly is feeling.

"Hi Mo!" he says to my belly, using the baby nickname we've inexplicably adopted over the last three months.

It's no dramatic romantic interaction, but we can't all accompany our husbands to the Oscars all the time.

After Matt leaves, I start cooking Gwyneth's Chicken Milanese with Tomato and Avocado Salad. It's a good weeknight meal, and I eat in front of a DVR'd episode of *The Mindy Project*. ("In my free time I prefer to do nothing but sit on the couch and watch TV," Beyoncé told *InStyle*. Me too!)

After dinner, I indulge myself in a mini-Beyoncé dance session before sitting back at the computer. I have two major deadlines this week, plus a backlog of emails to return, and I need a shot of energy.

At 10 P.M. I shut down my work and pull up YouTube. Time for some Jennifer Aniston yoga and Gwyneth Paltrow arm exercises. I do them in front of an episode of *Survivor* because, yes, I still watch more than twenty-five seasons later. The exercises last about the length of the TV show, and afterward I change and get into bed, where Matt is already sleeping.

My mental tally says I hit most of my marks. I could start juicing at home, or cut down even more on the toxins, or meditate longer, but overall it was a good day on the celebrity checklist front. I certainly don't feel perfect, but I feel better than I did seven months ago. I don't go to sleep thinking of all the things I should have done and didn't, which is a major improvement. I'm tired in an "I got a lot done" sort of way rather than just feeling sluggish and gross.

On its face, this was a very ordinary day, especially since I had no big plans—no meetings, no dinner dates, no doctor's appointments, no errands. Exercise, get dressed, work, eat, meditate, work, chat with husband, eat, work, exercise, sleep. It's nothing extraordinary, and it would be quite luxurious for many women. No fighting traffic to get to work, no kids to shuttle back and forth, no appointments to which to run late.

But that's the point. I didn't start this journey so that my life would suddenly look more fascinating on paper. I didn't expect that a few Gwyneth-inspired meals or Jennifer-based workouts would suddenly earn me a spot on the red carpet or in the pages of *People*. I wanted to feel more together and more in control, and by extension, happier. I wanted to placate the perfectionism that felt nearly paralyzing. I yearned for the confidence and sense of accomplishment that I perceived in the celebrities, even when they were just pumping gas or grocery shopping. While I would have loved to finish the year as Jennifer Aniston's doppelgänger, I didn't expect that to come true.

What did come to pass, though, was my desire for a sense of structure. Some people thrive in a go-with-the-flow lifestyle. Clearly I'm not one of them. A year ago, I got laid off. Suddenly each day was mine to schedule. I could sleep in. I could wear pajamas all day. I was lucky to be able to continue my career as a writer, but when a deadline wasn't looming I wasn't sure what to do with myself. I had all the time in the world, but I wasn't getting anything done. I felt schlumpy, and the pages of my favorite magazines and websites taunted me, as if solely there to remind me how unfabulous I was.

I'll never have the life of a celebrity. I'll never have the money, the access, the fans, the fame. I'll never know if these women I hold up as role models are in fact happy, or if the pressure of it all weighs on them at night. I can't know if they love the constant limelight, or hate it. But I know they'll never go away, and that we can use the celebrity bombardment as a reason to feel not good enough, or as inspiration to become better versions of ourselves. Our perception of celebrities, and of ourselves, is our reality.

In another twenty-six weeks, all the control and structure and I've-got-it-together-ness I've cultivated will disappear more quickly than it came. I'll be a disheveled mess—short on sleep and on exercise, forty pounds larger—and this perfect day will seem like a lifetime ago. I'll probably be as far from perfect as I've ever known.

I can't wait.

It's a girl!

Maggie Louise was born eleven weeks ago. Six pounds, eleven ounces; nineteen inches long. Healthy, happy, adorable.

Before we started trying to get pregnant, Matt said he hoped we never had a daughter. He didn't want her to inherit my perfectionism, he said, or be as hard on herself as I've been on myself. There are a million reasons I launched this project, but that might be at the core of it all. More than I wanted perfection, or glamour, or to feel fabulous, I wanted a child. And now I want to teach that child to be happy with who she is. I need her to know there's a difference between striving to be better and holding yourself to impossible standards.

Since Maggie arrived, my celebrity-inspired tasks—cute outfits, meditation, home-cooked meals—have taken a backseat to breast-feeding, diapers, and sleep. I'm usually in leggings and a T-shirt, I've barely worn makeup in the past three months, and I can hardly return an email let alone get Tina Fey levels of work done. As suspected, structured days have gone out the window—Maggie's whims dictate the days' activities, and she's not yet on a schedule. Some days she'll sleep, eat, and play in a predictable pattern; other days she'll cry uncontrollably for no apparent reason and calming her down is a mom-dad-and-grandma team effort.

I've said all along that striving for perfection is at odds with the pursuit of motherhood. But it depends on your definition of perfection. If it means wrinkle-free shirts and a six-pack, then the two can't necessarily co-exist. At least not when you have a new baby. Now my perfect day looks different than it did seven months ago. If Maggie eats well, gets through her witching hour without too much fuss, and gives us a decent night's sleep, I call it a win. If I shower and get in a quick workout, that's the new perfect.

But I'm not completely enlightened. I haven't blocked out all the celebrity noise. The "body after baby" messages haunt me— I've lost only two-thirds of the thirty-seven pounds I gained while pregnant, despite my ten-week weight-loss goal. "The idea that you should shed your baby bump in six weeks is bubbe meise," said my OB-GYN, using the Yiddish term for an old wives' tale. It will probably take more like six months, he told me, but I'm still mad at myself for holding on to these newly expanded hips and extra belly flab. I've seen enough *Us Weekly* covers of a post-partum Kourtney Kardashian to know that immediate weight loss is possible.

The other day I was gazing at a *Vogue* cover featuring an impeccably formed Gisele eight weeks postpartum when Matt caught me. "That makes sense," he said. "You should definitely compare yourself to the highest-paid supermodel in the world."

I know, and try to remind myself, that Gisele or the Kardashians or Kate Middleton or any superstar who makes the early days of motherhood look glamorous have help. Lots and lots of help. Nannies, trainers, chefs, more nannies. There's a reason they've never been caught in public with milk leaking through their T-shirt, as I was at the drugstore last week. But as has been the case throughout this project, even though I know intellectually that the stars don't come by their glamorous appearances easily or cheaply, I still want to live up to their examples.

On the surface, it may look like the efforts of the last year were for naught. One year later and I'm heavier than I was when I started. I'm not cooking, I'm covered in spit-up, and I'm still comparing myself to celebrities whose lifestyles are unrealistic for a layperson like me. But this project got me ready to turn my life upside down—it got me to a place of enough contentedness and confidence that I've been able to survive sleep deprivation, projectile poops, and the momentary loss of freedom without too many emotional breakdowns. I shudder to think what would have happened had Maggie arrived back when I was feeling lethargic, glued to the couch, and generally not-so-great about myself. The inevitable backslide that occurs when sleep comes in three-hour spurts and your baby cries every evening from 5:30–7:30 would have taken me to the dark place. Thanks to Gwyneth, Julia, the Jennifers et al, I don't feel guilty about this time of chaos. It's part of the journey, and I know that in a few weeks, when Maggie's in day care and we establish our new normal, I can dip into my arsenal of celebrity guidelines and reinstate the ones that worked for me. I'll dress in a presentable outfit (maybe even dust off that tutu), take some meditative breaths, and cook myself a healthy meal. I'll be the best version of myself—a nice treat for me, but a necessity for Maggie.

Matt is in love with our daughter. I'm sure he still worries that she'll inherit some of my Type-A tendencies, but I hope I've proven I'll do more good than harm. Every night before bed, I sing her a lullaby: "Just One Person" from *Snoopy!!! The Musical*. It's an entire song about believing in yourself, and I'm hoping that message will resonate deeper with Maggie than any tabloid headline. But just to be safe, I've resolved not to lament my body or my wardrobe or be too hard on myself in her presence.

One day, I'll encourage Maggie to have role models, and we'll talk about the aspects of the stars we admire, and why. Maybe we'll flip through the pages of *Us Weekly* together. Or *Sports Illustrated*. Or *Time*. Hopefully all three. By then I like to think we'll both feel so fabulous and put-together and happy with ourselves that we'll look to these magazines for entertainment and information rather than as a standard of living. It's a tall order but a worthy goal.

I'm no closer to being a celebrity than I was when I started this project, but that was never the point. I'll never have Sarah Jessica's wardrobe, but I'm a few steps closer to her confidence. I may not be as Zen as Julia or as successful as Tina, but with their help I've figured out how to harness my energy for calm and productivity.

Our little family will never end up in the pages of *People,* but our trips to the park will be just as loving as the Affleck-Garners'.

They'll be perfect.

LIVING THE CELEBRITY LIFE
(WITH A REGULAR PERSON'S TIME AND MONEY):

A Handy Guide

Health and Fitness

- **Try YouTube.** You may not have access to—let alone the money for—fancy personal trainers. Luckily, many celebrity trainers have short exercise videos posted for free online. Search Mandy Ingber (trainer to Jennifer Aniston), Tracy Anderson (Gwyneth), Gunnar Peterson (Sofia Vergara, Jennifer Lopez), and Haley Pasternak (Rihanna, Halle Berry) for superstar-caliber workouts at no cost.

- **Barter for services.** Gyms, yoga studios, and Pilates classes can be pricey. Especially if you are exercising the celebrity-mandated five or six times a week. Plenty of studios offer free classes in exchange for a few hours a week of checking in clients, cleaning, or watching kids.

- **"Don't eat shit."** Interpret them as you will, but Jennifer Aniston's words will have you rethinking your decision to eat that donut or to microwave that frozen "diet" meal.

- **Keep light weights in the house.** Jennifer Aniston and Beyoncé both say they lift in front of the TV or during a favorite song. Their arms speak for themselves.

Kitchen

- **Try the farmer's market.** Walking home from the market, fresh tomatoes and mozzarella in tow, will inevitably make you feel fabulous. It's very *Us Weekly*, and Gwyneth-approved.

- **Get a blender.** Smoothies are the celebrity health food of choice, but can be pricey for an everyday snack or breakfast meal. Throw ice, some fruit, and veggies in a blender and you'll be en route to eating like a star. Skip the green powders, unless you're braver than I am.
- **Throw a dinner party.** Invite friends over, use your cloth napkins, and serve three courses. Your name will reek of glamour.

Fashion

- **Mix high and low.** Just look at the tabloid photos—celebrities have a knack for mixing fancy garb with casual pieces to look stylish without seeming overdressed. Try pairing a white T-shirt with heels, or ripped jeans with your favorite purse.
- **Befriend an employee.** Whether she works at Bloomingdale's, The Gap, or your favorite local boutique, a fashion professional has an invaluable eye. Getting input from someone in the industry is the average girl's version of having a personal stylist.
- **Take a risk with a statement piece.** As Tim Gunn advises, choose only one. Mine is a tutu, yours might be red leather boots. Just make sure it's something you love.
- **When all else is too much work, go with sunglasses and lip gloss.** Per Beyoncé. She knows of what she speaks.

Career

- **Don't wait for long stretches of time.** If you wait for an uninterrupted stretch of three hours before diving into a project, you'll be waiting forever.
- **Remember you can't do everything.** To get ahead in one area, you might have to sacrifice another. Tina Fey sacrifices exercise; I often sacrifice a home-cooked meal. When work is especially busy, cut yourself some slack.

- **Learn to let go.** Do your best work, then turn it in. If you pore over a project forever, you'll never move on to the next one.
- **Say no. But only sometimes.** Shouldering multiple commitments may make you feel like you're conquering the world, but don't overextend yourself. Err on the side of saying yes, but be realistic. Say no when saying yes would compromise the caliber of your work.

Marriage

- **Embrace one of his interests.** Sports, poker, video games. Immerse yourself in one of his hobbies and you may even take a liking to it yourself.
- **Speak only kindly in public.** Quit the light jabs at his expense. If you wouldn't want it quoted in *Us Weekly*, keep it to yourself (or your very best friends).
- **Hold on to your girlfriends.** Maintaining strong relationships outside your marriage will help at home. As Jennifer Garner says, you won't mind too much if your husband is constantly working—as long as you have friends to bitch about it to. (Plus you can go on those girlfriend getaways *People* is always writing about.)
- **Surprise him.** "Be the woman he knows with a little bit of a twist," says Beyoncé. Whatever that means to you.

Serenity

- **Meditate.** It works for so many celebrities, or so they claim. Twenty minutes a day is ideal. Five is fine, too.
- **Cut down on social media.** Julia Roberts's whole "I've never seen a Facebook page" seems drastic, but cutting back on your screen time will help you be present.
- **Write a gratitude list.** A journal works best, but even a one-

time dose of thankfulness will help you attain Julia's sense of fulfillment.

- **Take a staycation, even if only for an hour.** Beyoncé suggests a day spa or winery, but an hour-long massage or solo lunch outing might be more your speed (and price point). It'll do the trick.

Pregnancy

- **Pamper yourself.** Do it before you're too busy pampering a baby. Take a bubble bath, do your makeup, take a nap.
- **Cut down on toxins.** Eliminating them entirely is a tall order—but doable, if you're dedicated. Jessica Alba provides a list of offending chemicals in the back of *The Honest Life* (and plenty alternatives for purchase through The Honest Company). Otherwise try to avoid: brominated flame retardants, phthalates, petroleum, bleach, formaldehyde, pesticides, mercury, and bisphenol A (BPA).
- **Dress the bump.** Alba suggests fitted shirts (with long sweaters to cover your growing backside), V-necks, and long necklaces. The more you try to hide the belly, the more frumpy—and less fabulous—you'll look and feel.
- **Enjoy your last moments of being a kid.** Soon you'll have one of your own. For now, sleep late, go to the movies, and "take care of [your] childlike self."

ACKNOWLEDGMENTS

A big thank-you to my wonderful agent, Kari Stuart at ICM, who seems to love both books and celebrity culture as much as I do, and always knows just when to cheer me on. Thanks also to Alison Schwartz, who understood what this quest was about even before I did.

Jennifer Smith is such a smart, kind, and insightful editor, and never writes me off when I have absurd questions or concerns. This book is infinitely better because of you, and I am so grateful. Thanks, too, to Hannah Elnan, who kept this book moving along, kept me on schedule, and was incredibly understanding when the chaos of new motherhood threw me off deadline.

Also at Ballantine, thanks to Libby McGuire, Jennie Tung, Richard Callison, Alison Masciovecchio, Maggie Oberrender, and everyone who has supported this book from day one.

Thanks to Jake Halpern, Dr. Alice Domar, and Becky Gillespie for sharing their expertise.

Thanks to Lauren Miller for being the world's best sounding board. Who knew a "blog friend" could turn into one of my most invaluable readers?

I should probably thank the celebrities who have inspired this quest. While they don't know me, I certainly feel like I know them. This self-improvement journey would not have been possible without their glowing and glamorous appearances in my favorite magazines.

My mother and brother, Harriet Bertsche and Alex Bertsche, are so supportive, and I'm eternally grateful that they encourage my projects and actually seem happy to read my every draft. Thanks also to Jane Levine and the entire Levine-Bertsche-Epstein clan.

Thanks to the wonderful doctors who helped me reach my most important goal over the course of this year. You gave me the best gift one can give.

To Maggie, I hope this book gives you a glimpse into just how much I love you.

And the biggest thank-you of all goes to my husband, Matt, who listens to me complain that I don't have Beyoncé's body and stands by as I take on one self-improvement project after another, and loves me just the same. You are the best.